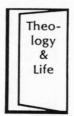

Theo-
logy
&
Life

THEOLOGY AND LIFE SERIES

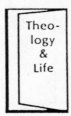

Volume 32

The Rise of the Papacy

by

Robert B. Eno, S.S.

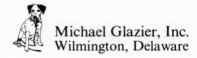

Michael Glazier, Inc.
Wilmington, Delaware

About the Author

Robert B. Eno, S.S., holds his doctorate in theology from Institute Catholique de Paris. His work in ecumenical and historical studies is widely recognized, and he has devoted much research to the focal question of doctrinal authority. He is a professor of church history at the Catholic University of America.

First published in 1990 by Michael Glazier, Inc., 1935 West Fourth Street, Wilmington, Delaware 19805.

Library of Congress Cataloging-in-Publication Data

Eno, Robert B.
    The rise of the papacy/ by Robert B. Eno.
      p. cm.—(Theology and life series: 32)
    "Tuohy lectures"—Introd.
    Includes bibliographical references.
    ISBN 0-89453-802-0
    1. Papacy—History—To 1309. 2. Church history—Primitive and early church, ca. 30-600. 3. Catholic Church—Doctrines—History. I. Title. II. Title: Tuohy lectures. III. Series.
BX970.E56   1990
262'.13'09015—dc20
                                        90-34222
                                        CIP

Typography by Brenda Belizzone
Printed in the U.S. by St. Mary's Press

Contents

꙲

Preface

John Carroll University has an endowed chair, the Walter and Mary Tuohy Chair of Interreligious Studies, which brings to the campus distinguished visiting scholars to give classes and lectures on topics of ecumenical and interreligious interest. This chair honors two prominent Clevelanders who were committed to ecumenism.

Few topics have as much significance for the ecumenical movement as the papacy. During the Reformation the Protestants accused the popes of having manufactured out of whole cloth their authority and power in the Church; the popes responded by claiming that their power derived from Saint Peter himself and had always been recognized in the Church. While the tone and tenor of the debate have moderated since the Reformation, the place of the papacy in the Christian Church remains a major issue for anyone interested in ecumenism, and it is a fitting subject for the Tuohy Chair.

We can discard the sixteenth-century framework—no one today seriously claims the papacy emerged as the result of a centuries-long machinations nor, on the other hand, does anyone seriously claim that the papacy's claims have always been recognized by all Christians. But the question still remains: how did the bishopric of Rome, prominent but initially no more prominent than other important bishoprics such as Alexandria or Antioch, rise to the position it enjoyed in the Middle Ages and, for Roman Catholics, well beyond?

The chapters in this book, based upon public lectures given at the university, deal with this crucial question. The author and the Tuohy Fellow for 1987-1988, Robert B. Eno, s.s., of the Catholic University of America, is a leading authority on the papacy as well as an active participant in ecumenical affairs, specifically the Lutheran-Roman Catholic Dialogue. He brings to the question his considerable scholarship as well as his concern for the Church of today. His stay at John Carroll University is well-remembered; Robert is a good teacher, colleague, and raconteur. He is also a fine lecturer, and we at JCU are pleased to make his (revised) lectures available to a wide audience.

Joseph F. Kelly, Director
The Walter and Mary Tuohy Chair of
Interreligious Studies, John Carroll
University, Cleveland, Ohio

Introduction

In November of 1985, while I was on sabbatical in Berkeley, California, Professor Joseph Kelly of John Carroll University wrote to invite me to come to Cleveland for the Fall semester of 1987 to hold the Walter and Mary Tuohy Chair of Inter-religious Studies at that university and to deliver the lecture series attached to the Chair. He suggested that I take as my subject the history of the ancient Papacy. This is an area in which I had been interested since the early 1970s when I had participated in a subcommittee of the Lutheran-Roman Catholic Dialogue, then engaged on the topic of the Roman primacy. By 1976, when I became a full member of the Dialogue group, the subject under discussion had moved on to the related issue of teaching authority and infallibility. Over the years at the Catholic University of America, from time to time, I have offered a course which reviews the relevant texts and issues.

The Tuohy Lectures as presented here in slightly enlarged form are not meant to be a complete history of the ancient Papacy. Rather they have a two-fold general aim: first, to illustrate the complexity of the issues, the numerous unknowns and uncertainties, found in the earliest centuries. Answers are not as simple as they may seem to partisans of one side or the other. Second, in the last three lectures, in particular, I have sought to emphasize that, once Roman documentation becomes abundant, the Roman drive toward centralization is clear and unrelenting. In pursuit of the second goal, a detailed study is made of the Roman letters. Thus the problems currently being debated about "the limits of the Papacy" or the theological foundation for the authority of episcopal conferences have their roots in very old dilemmas.

I wish to thank Professor Joseph Kelly for inviting me to hold the Tuohy Chair and to deliver these lectures, as well as President Thomas O'Malley, S.J., of John Carroll University,

Professor Kelly and the faculty of the department of religious studies for their hospitality and cordiality in making me feel welcome. My actual "home away from home" was with the Jesuit community of Rodman Hall with whom I lived and enjoyed a pleasant semester.

I hope that these lectures will at least show the extent of the problems facing ecumenists, if not contribute much to the solution.

Robert B. Eno, S.S.

I

The Beginnings

Catholicae ecclesiae episcopus, Bishop of the Catholic Church. Such was the title used by Pope Paul VI as he signed the documents of the Second Vatican Council. As D. H. Marot[1] explains in his study of the episcopal vocabulary in the fifth to the seventh centuries, the original phrase used by a Roman bishop went back to the fifth century and was "bishop of the Catholic church of the city of Rome." It had also been used earlier to distinguish the Catholic bishop from the bishop of a dissident group in the same city.

But some might see in such a title an unintended statement about the real state of the Church. "Bishop of the Catholic Church": Has not the bishop of Rome become in practice the one and only real bishop in the Catholic Church? The bishop whose powers, "ordinary and immediate" as the First Vatican Council termed them, reach out to every diocese, every parish, indeed every Catholic in the world? Have not the other bishops become little more than local agents for the one real bishop? Such suggestions were clearly and ominously heard after the First Vatican Council.[2] But many at the time also predicted that there would never be another ecumenical council either. Given papal infallibility, why spend all that money and waste the time of thousands of bishops when Rome makes all the decisions anyway? Then came the Second Vatican Council and the hoped-for theological redressing of the balance between the Papacy and episcopacy.

But one council does not annul its predecessors; on the

* Notes for this chapter can be found on pp. 151-53

contrary, it reaffirms them, and in *Lumen Gentium* Vatican II did reiterate the ecclesiological determinations of Vatican I. All such conciliar documents necessarily represent certain compromises, thus leaving passages in the various documents which future divergent parties can cite as favoring their own views and interpretations.[3] The two ecclesiologies of Vatican II[4] leave an increasingly problematic legacy both for ourselves and future generations. The years following the council have shown that the problem of papal-episcopal relations is far from resolved. In fact, some would argue that after a brief and modest experiment with decentralization, centralizing tendencies have returned with a vengeance. Rome can be consulted now almost in a matter of minutes from any part of the world. Bishops and others can and do go to Rome in person, frequently with a journey of only a few hours. And now, if you cannot go to Rome, the Pope will come to you. In other words, modern means of communication and travel have made centralization easier than ever.

Within Vatican II's notion of the "hierarchy of truths,"[5] the institution of the Papacy, as one instrument of Church governance, may seem fairly peripheral in relation to the central truths of the faith concerning God and Christ. But in fact we know that this is not the case in practice. Pope Paul VI honestly and courageously admitted that his office, meant to promote and preserve the unity of the Church, in fact too often has been the very stumbling block which has prevented that unity from being realized. The visits of Pope John Paul II to our own country make it useful to present this study of the early centuries of this institution, the Papacy, so central to the life of Western civilization. And one recurring secondary theme will be that of centralization as a constant in the structural development of the Church over the centuries.

In the seventeenth century, the latitudinarian Anglican William Chillingworth[6] wrote a book whose thesis at least became well-known: The Bible and only the Bible is the Religion of Protestants. Sometimes it may seem that for some Catholics the Pope and the Pope alone is their religion. While I do not agree with von Balthasar[7] that Papolatry is not always with us, Catholics in fact professing unconditional loyalty to

Rome can be remarkably selective in what or in whom they choose to support and extol. Hans Küng continually cites John XXIII as his ideal Pope. On the other side, some radical conservative groups refuse to acknowledge any legitimate Pope after Pius XII. One group on the lunatic fringe claimed that Paul VI had been kidnapped and was being held prisoner in Spain while an impostor, his face altered by the most skillful plastic surgeons, held forth in the Vatican, promulgating all manner of heresies, no doubt.[8] We used to have appeals from the Pope to the ecumenical council; now we can have appeals from the impostor Pope to the real one, whereever you are! Less radical commentators who trumpet forth their undying support for every Roman pronouncement conceived of as conservative on matters of dogma and morals, especially sexual morality, yawn and look the other way when matters of social or economic justice are treated. William Buckley led the way when, after John XXIII's encyclical *Mater et Magistra* was published in 1961, he commented, "Mater Si; Magistra, No." This is no novel development, as we shall see. For example, the North African bishops of the fifth century, after angrily rejecting Pope Zosimus' seeming approval of Pelagius and Celestius, announced that they were standing firm with his predecessor's condemnation of the same.

Recent Literature on Peter

Our purpose here is to study the early historical development of the Roman primacy in the early Church. In so doing, one must clearly give some account of the role of Peter, the Cephas of history and the Peter of faith. Among post-World War II studies, that of Oscar Cullmann, *Peter: Disciple, Apostle, Martyr* (1952)[9] found New Testament evidence for a leadership role for Peter among the Twelve. But even this role was ephemeral, claimed Cullmann, and was given up when Peter left Jerusalem to devote himself fully to the mission to the Jews of the Diaspora, leaving James of Jerusalem in a position of leadership for the Church. Like many other such studies, Cullmann's finds some role of leadership for Peter in the early days but, even if such leadership be considered an office, no evidence whatsoever is found for any kind of succession in such an office (p. 230). Like the apostolic ministry itself, Peter's role of leadership among the Twelve, however conceived, was something definitively limited to the earliest generation of those who had been the witnesses of Jesus' resurrection.

The most recent wave of studies is typified by the best-known of them, *Peter in the New Testament* (1973).[10] This joint study by Roman Catholic and Protestant scholars has been very influential and has been translated into several languages. It was a by-product of the U.S.A. National Lutheran-Roman Catholic Dialogue which from 1970-73 discussed the topic of Roman Primacy. A special scriptural panel of Catholic and Lutheran exegetes, some full members of the Dialogue group and other invited scholars, including one Anglican and one Reformed, met to seek an exegetical consensus of how Catholic and non-Catholic interpreters view the person and work of Peter in the New Testament.

The outstanding feature here, seen necessarily in the studies which came after, was to avoid simply lumping all the books of the New Testament together to arrive at a single New Testament portrait of Peter. It was realized and admitted here that the New Testament is made up of a considerable variety of traditions, each of which must be studied separately if one hopes to finish with a reasonably accurate overall picture. So, there is no one New Testament portrait of Peter; there are several traditions, in some of which Peter is more prominent; in others, less so. So it is thus admitted that the New Testament itself and the earliest Christian traditions pre-existing the written Scriptures, while not so numerous, chaotic and self-contradictory as some radical scholars like Walter Bauer[11] had argued, were not as homogeneous and clear, not as uniform a whole from the very start, as most believers had usually assumed.

Even if all the scholars of this panel had agreed upon all the various New Testament traditions and schools, that would not mean that the same scholars would therefore have a uniform evaluation of how Peter was viewed in each tradition. Indeed the convergences of *Peter in the New Testament* are accordingly modest, "a cautious minimum" (p. 58), stating that Peter was prominent among the disciples (p. 159), that is, the historical Peter at least as portrayed by the evangelists of different traditions. "Peter was the most important of the Twelve in Jerusalem and its environs" (p. 161); a guardian against false teaching (p. 166) as, for example, when in the Second Letter of Peter the Peter image is used to warn against certain dangerous misinterpretations of Paul (p. 167). (The letters of Peter were not written by the historical Peter.) "There is a plurality of images associated with Peter" (p. 166) in early Christian thought. The Petrine trajectory, as they refer to it, does not and cannot take one very far and the scholars gathered for *Peter in the New Testament* pass the ball on to the patristic scholars.

A more recent study, *Petrine Controversies in Early Christianity,*[12] by the British Protestant scholar Terence Smith, published in Tübingen in 1985, proceeds in similar fashion, though perhaps with greater attention paid to the Apocrypha. His concern is also primarily with Peter's image (rather than with the historical Peter). What do the various groups make of Peter or how do they use or perhaps misuse his memory especially, as the title indicates, in controversy with other Christian groups? He concludes to an extraordinary flexibility of the Petrine image so that it was far from being the exclusive property of orthodox Christian groups, especially in the second century. Indeed, he claims that "there is an astonishing lack of reference to Peter among ecclesiastical authors of the first half of the second century. He is barely mentioned in the Apostolic Fathers, nor by Justin and the other Apologists" (p. 214).

The most significant Roman Catholic study since the joint *Peter in the New Testament* would be Rudolf Pesch's *Simon-Petrus*[13] of 1980. Here I am not concerned with his detailed study of Peter in the various New Testament traditions but in his general conclusions. Pesch concludes, among other things, that neither the story of the historical Peter nor the image of Peter in the later New Testament traditions is of *immediate* importance for the primacy of the Roman bishops. Indeed, later references back to Peter in the New Testament, primarily Matthew 16:18, may sometimes appear almost to be an afterthought. For Pesch, an issue such as a general leadership of the Church is an open question. Even if Peter is conceived as a sort of leader among the Twelve, whether his "Petrine office," if there was such a thing, had successors is also an open question. Even if one could directly argue for such a successor on the basis of the New Testament text, there remains the most elusive and fascinating question of all: Is there a missing link in the first and second centuries between the historical Peter and a bishop of Rome conceived of as a successor to him?

The destruction of Jerusalem in 70 A.D. and again in 135 helped to pave the way for the rise of another center for world Christianity, Rome. This also, of course, helps to explain the surprisingly minor role played by Jerusalem in that early history. But Pesch's views and such considerations nevertheless leave us with the intriguing hypothesis that neither the historical Peter nor Peter's image in the first and second century had the decisive role to play in the initial rise of the Roman see to a position of leadership in the world Church. Hence the question of the development of Church office within the local Christian church and the origin of the monarchical episcopate, above all in the Roman Christian community, emerge unexpectedly as key issues for the study of the beginnings of Roman primacy. Perhaps then the only reason why *Peter in the New Testament* failed to come to any decisive conclusion was that no such conclusion was possible from the study of the New Testament alone. As we saw, these New Testament scholars themselves urged that the question be passed on to patristic specialists. I must confess that there is probably where it belongs.

More a patristic than a biblical question.

Peter in Rome

Before carrying that issue further, we should at least review quickly the current consensus concerning the historical Peter's role in Rome itself, though, to be sure, it is largely based on conjecture and later Roman traditions. Since the Reformation, many have sought to contest the massive Petrine tradition of the Christian church of the city of Rome. So much so that some scholars have claimed that the historical Peter never came anywhere near Rome. The Protestant scholar Karl Heussi is a recent example of an opponent of Peter's presence in Rome. (Cf. the survey of the debate in Cullmann, pp. 71-7).

Current consensus,[14] however, is much more positive, arguing that Peter and Paul were in Rome. And if in Rome, it is not unreasonable to see them exercising a position of leadership in the Christian community there. They died in Rome as martyrs, probably during the persecution of Nero. Finally, they were buried in Rome so that, especially in later centuries, the possession of the relics of Peter and Paul would be of great, even decisive importance. The erection of the Constantinian basilicas, on the Vatican Hill for Peter and on the road to Ostia outside the city walls for Paul, shows that the Roman Christians of that time believed that the remains of the Apostles had been buried on those sites. The difficulty of building the original St. Peter's Basilica on a hill and in the midst of a cemetery further strengthens the foundation of the belief concerning Peter's burial place. A Roman priest named Gaius referred *circa* 200 to the *tropaia* of the Apostles in the same places.[15] The precise meaning of *tropaia* has been debated but most would agree that it probably refers to some modest monument placed over the burial places of the Apostles. Purists may claim that this proves nothing except that *circa* 200 the Roman church believed that these were the burial places of Peter and Paul. Most would not find it a strain on their credulity to give such a tradition the benefit of any doubt. Traditions about such important sites, after all, could be preserved for many generations, and when it became feasible, when the persecutions had ceased for a while, simple memorials could have been raised over the places of burial. Thus, in all likelihood, the main altar of the current St. Peter's Basilica does still rise over the remains of the Apostle Peter who ended his long journey from Galilee to the center of the Roman Empire by dying as a witness to his Lord.

Whether, as Pope Paul VI once asserted, we can point out the actual bones is much more problematic. The work of the excavators and researchers of the 1940s and 1950s, especially that of Professor Margherita Guarducci, has been severely criticized, and the whole issue is much more debatable and uncertain than the recent popularized account of John Walsh (*The Bones of St. Peter,* 1982) would indicate.

Two further details need to be pointed out: Was Peter the "founder" of the Church in Rome? Paul clearly could not have been since he wrote his letter to the Romans to an already existing Christian community in Rome which he was proposing to visit. If by founder is meant that Peter was the first preacher of Christianity in Rome, then Peter should not be called the founder. He no doubt also arrived in a pre-existing Christian community in Rome. But they, Peter and Paul, are still considered the founders, the foundational stones, of the Roman Church in a moral, if not absolutely literal, historical sense.

Secondly, was Peter the first bishop of Rome? Such a designation originates in an ill-conceived collapsing of the unique role of the apostle into the later Church office of bishop. Such an identification of founding apostle and first bishop (of any apostolic see) is found, for example, in Cyprian in the mid-third century. But it is an anachronism; the earliest bishop-lists do not consider the founding apostle simply as the first bishop. There is the founding apostle (for example, Mark in Alexandria) and after him comes the first bishop, again expressing the essential difference between the two roles and the constitutive significance of the foundational generation over against the episcopal succession for the rest of time and all the other generations which come after.[16] So in that technical but nevertheless very important sense, Peter was not the first bishop of Rome. The little known Linus holds that honor. Peter was more important than that. Needless to add, most of the episcopal and papal paraphernalia later centuries purported to associate with Peter—mitres, episcopal thrones and the like—are obviously anachronisms.

The Structures of the Local Church

Let us turn then to what very well may be more significant for the development of Roman primacy—the development of the offices of ministry and leadership within the local church.[17] In recent decades, especially because of the ecumenical movement, this has been a subject of intense interest and research. And Catholic scholars, probably the good majority of them at least, have come to accept the fundamental conclusion that the basic leadership structure of bishop-presbyter-deacon, the so-called apostolic ministry, is not as such the product of dominical institution or, to put it simply, such offices were not instituted explicitly by Jesus during his earthly ministry. Rather, the argument goes, local structures developed in various ways and at different rates of speed in different places in the Church so that only *circa* 175 could it be seen as a universal form of local ministerial structure in the world Church.

The literature is so extensive on this and the arguments so complex that we cannot here go into all the details. But the literature of the first century and a good deal for the first half of the second century does not indicate the existence of a single individual, the bishop, in a clear leadership position in the local church. The titles are already in the New Testament itself but that does not prove that the presumed later structures and configuration of ministries were there. Likewise, there are many gaps in our knowledge; no doubt the offices can be found in one community at a certain time or at another time in another community. But I do not think that such a fact authorizes us to project some desired picture of uniformity back on to the first decades.

In his 1967 book, *The Church,* Hans Küng portrayed (for example, p. 403 of the English edition) the Christian community of Corinth at a certain point in its earliest history as "charismatic," without a clear structural organization. He was much criticized for this, though he was not proposing this as either the original form of all Christian communities, still less as some ideal form, but simply as a passing phase whose very anarchical results themselves showed the undeniable need for structured authority.[18] But it does help to show, along with much other evidence, that the bishop-presbyter-deacon structure is not *de iure divino* and therefore, theoretically at least, can give place to other forms of ministry and Church government.

Any question will yield varying answers depending on the starting position and the premises. Our inquiry presumes that it is necessary that the Christian Church have an organized ministry, one of whose tasks is to structure and lead the local community. There can be a great variety of Church structures, but they cannot be totally eliminated with the expectation that the community will survive with any recognizable unity and identity. The Roman primacy belongs primarily to the level of structures which deal with relations between and among the local churches. But first must come the question of the leadership structure within the local church. As I have indicated, one cannot presume *a priori* that from some pre-existent blueprint of divine or apostolic origins, come the precise offices of ministers for each local congregation.

No one has ever offered the definitive answer to the question: When and where did the various structural configurations emerge? Some have held that the offices with functional names (*episkopos* = overseer; *diakonos* = servant or minister) came from Greek communities, whereas presbyters or elders originated in Jewish communities. But this neat distinction was brought into question by the Dead Sea Scrolls and the office mentioned there of an overseer of the Qumran Essene community. Indeed, the closest thing one finds to a monarchical bishop in the first century is precisely the role of James in the Jewish Christian community of Jerusalem. Yet this arrangement is unique in its own way as well. The successors of James were to come from the blood relatives of Jesus or their descendants. This unusual requirement could not last and in fact the Jewish Christians of Jerusalem are soon replaced by a Christian community of Gentile origin there.

The titles *episkopos,* presbyter, and deacon existed in the first century.[19] But the relationships among the three offices (or at least between the first two) are not clear. Did all communities have *episkopoi?* If so, were there two or three or more in the leadership group? Were all the presbyters *episkopoi?* Were there some communities which had only one *episkopos* and if so, how much authority did he have? Are the titles *episkopoi* and *presbyteroi* universally interchangeable or are they merely linked? Obviously the picture in the New

Testament is not clear. What is clear there is the trend toward greater authority for the leadership group. This is already unmistakable in the Pastoral epistles. The threat of the centrifugal forces which pull apart the unity of the congregation, especially the threat of false teachers and teachings, points to the need for a solution and, more often than not, that solution points in the direction of giving more authority to community leaders, whoever they may be. Cf. Titus 1:5ff., where "Paul" gives the counsel to Titus to appoint elders in every town but goes on to delineate the spiritual requirements for a "bishop." 1 Timothy 3 also describes the requirements for a bishop and also for a deacon. No mention of elders is made at the point but at 5:17 the group of community leaders (presumably the same group) are collectively referred to as presbyters. In Acts 20, Paul, upon leaving Miletus, calls the elders together to bid them goodbye and in his address refers to them as *episkopoi* (Acts 20:28). This same ambiguity (from the point of view of the modern reader) persists in many of the non-canonical writings of the late first and early second centuries called the Apostolic Fathers.

The Apostolic Fathers

Two of this group of texts are of particular interest here. Their dates have long been the source of dispute and no doubt will continue to be. The *Didache,* or "Teaching of the Twelve Apostles," may well mirror the situation of some local communities, even as early as the first century. Here, an older, itinerant ministry of apostles, prophets, and teachers appears to be fading: the prolonged discussions of the problem of false prophets; the difficulty of distinguishing the authentic preachers from the apparently growing number of pretenders and free-loaders (ch. 11). Chapter 15 seems to portray the process of transition from an itinerant ministry to a stable ministry taken from the local community which now chooses its own men to be bishops (plural) and deacons (no presbyters mentioned). As in the Pastoral Epistles, Christians are urged "Do not despise them." It was not to be presumed that one's next door neighbor, chosen to lead the local community, would automatically be able to command the respect and support of those who had known him all his life. The prophet is not without honor except in his own country.

Ignatius of Antioch

The other author we must look at, the decisive one, is Ignatius of Antioch,[20] bishop of Syria as he called himself, who died *circa* 112 or 116 A.D. He had been arrested in Antioch and was being brought to Rome for trial. He wrote six letters to local communities in Asia Minor through which he passed and one ahead to Rome, his final destination. The principal feature of these letters for our purposes is that for the first time there stands out clearly the figure of the single authoritative leader, the *episkopos*, the bishop. In these letters, one might almost use the word "ruler" as well as "leader" of the local Christian community. There is also a collegial group of elders whose role is not clear, though it seems to be more one of advising the bishop than of sharing his role as liturgist. The function of the deacons is even more undefined.

The classical structural configuration of the apostolic ministry for the first time stands out with great, albeit not total, definition. The very clarity of the figure of the monarchical bishop at this early date is at the root of why so many scholars, even today, question the authenticity of these letters or their dating. Could such a development stand out so clearly so early? We will say yes here and accept the early dating. These letters are among the most thoroughly studied of early patristic writings and without going into detail here, suffice it to say that the readers and hearers are again urged and exhorted to submit themselves to the bishop's leadership, his commands, and so forth, without question. Obey him. If you are not with the bishop, you are not with Christ. These early letters then constitute exhibit A in the onward march of structural centralization and concentration of authority within the Church. It must happen first within the local church before starting on a wider stage.

Assuming that the local church which Ignatius led had this clear-cut structure, one is not thereby authorized to conclude that this structure was now the general rule throughout the Church in the early second century. The opposite appears to be more likely. This leads most scholars to conclude that the situation Ignatius addressed was not one in which the monarchical episcopate was the universal rule in local churches. Rather, his strong statements functioned within a sort of campaign to promote what he thought the churches needed, namely, the prestige and authority of a single leader in the local community, such as Polycarp in Smyrna. Like the author of the Pastoral Epistles, Ignatius feared the disintegration of the local community because of Docetists and Judaizers, if there were not a strong leader who could command obedience, in whom the identity of the Church could be anchored and around whom the faithful could rally.

The Christian movement was threatened with the tendency to divide into splinter groups early on. Celsus, an early polemicist against Christianity, writing in the second half of the second century, already noted in his list of objections that Christians could not agree on anything.[21] So from an early time, measures developed to try to stabilize the mainstream. These included as one principal component the increasing authority placed in the hands of one man in the local community, the bishop. And so was established as the mainspring of self-protection, a strong centralizing movement, first in the local church, a trend that one local church in particular, the Catholic Church of the city of Rome, would bring to it fullest development on the world-wide scale and for basically the same reasons.

Other Means of Protecting the Apostolic Heritage

Other measures[22] developed concerning the multiplying sources by which the Lord's teachings reached Christians of later generations over the supply lines which grew ever longer with the passing decades. The confused thoughts attributed to Papias demonstrate well enough by themselves the increasing unreliability of the very oral tradition being extolled. Even written documents did not suffice, as the burgeoning number of apocryphal gospels, epistles, and apocalypses illustrates. On general principles, or perhaps especially in reaction against Marcion, who rejected the Jewish Scriptures and bowdlerized the New Testament, local churches drew up lists of written works they accepted as in conformity with the apostolic teaching as they understood it. Thus the origins of the canon of the New Testament.

But as all knew very well and as Tertullian effectively expressed in his *De praescriptione haereticorum,*[23] even canonical Scripture contained a great many contested texts whose meaning either was not clear or was debatable. Short statements of basic beliefs, deemed, to be sure, to be taken from the Scriptures were drawn up. These are the *regulae fidei*[24] found in a number of patristic texts, and they in turn are closely allied to the statements of faith associated with the baptismal ceremony. Such statements, by the way, were an integral part of a baptismal ceremony in which the baptismal form was not declaratory but a three-fold interrogation followed by a triple immersion, as in Hippolytus' *Apostolic Tradition* (Rome, *circa* 215 but claiming to represent a long-standing practice). Both of these forms of statements of belief soon developed into what we know as the Creeds.

As the early centuries of the Church demonstrate (not to mention the later centuries) doctrinal statements may be debated as hotly as biblical ones. Thus the inevitable recourse to a living teaching authority for the interpretation of debated texts. With the condemnation of Montanism[25] in the second century, a movement in Asia Minor which claimed that the charism of prophecy had not disappeared from the Church and that divine revelation had not ceased but was an ongoing reality, revelation could now more easily be envisaged as a reality that belonged to the receding past, a sort of keepsake from Christ and the Apostles, safely tucked away in the trunk, so to speak, for safe-keeping. Such a picture springs from the reigning metaphor, also found in the Pastoral Epistles, namely, the deposit of faith. Who were to be the privileged guardians of this apparently static reality? Primarily those same office holders who were now being recommended as the guardians of the unity of the local church—the bishops. They were to guard it and in the classic statement, add nothing to it and take nothing away from it.

Rome as the Apostolic See

As time went on, certain sees and consequently their bishops became more important in the world Church; I speak of what would later be termed the development of metropolitan sees and patriarchates.[26] I believe that it is within this context that Roman authority first developed significantly, with appeal to Petrine texts coming later as a support for this rise of Rome and its claim to be a universal arbiter and center of appeal for the Church. Rome was the sole local church of the western empire that could claim to be the foundation of an apostle and, of course, not just one apostle but two—and what a pair! The two outstanding apostles, Peter and Paul. And they had not simply passed through; they had preached and died as glorious martyrs. They were there permanently; they had come to stay. Their relics were there, first in relative obscurity and secrecy, but later at the center of magnificent settings. In the view of later centuries, the power of the saints was especially concentrated and localized in the place where their relics rested.[27] Other western cities of great population and wealth such as Carthage made no claim to be of apostolic origin. Rome was unique in the West. Its importance in the Christian Church was not tied directly or in any significant way to its civic and historic heritage though its importance and centrality obviously had something to do with the reason why Peter and Paul went there in the first place! They did not go to London or Paris!

The East, on the other hand, had many apostolic sees. Such a distinction there was of much less significance for being so commonplace. Thus it is not surprising that Eastern cities were given their rank in the Church primarily according to their civil importance,[28] the larger city that was also a provincial capital would also become the metropolitan see of the province, for example. This made possible periodic revision. If a city declined in importance or size or wealth, its ecclesiastical position might also be lost to another city. The different criteria for ecclesiastical significance between East and West would later lead to the longstanding confrontation between Rome and the East, especially over Rome's refusal to recognize the status of Constantinople as New Rome, the new imperial capital. Rather it was rejected as non-apostolic, an historical upstart and newcomer.

The Problem of Rome's Local Church Structure

If Rome's position is closely tied to the importance of its bishop, what would be the result of the discovery that there was a time when it did not have a bishop? I do not refer to some *sede vacante* period between the death of one bishop and the election of a new one but to the possibility that in the late first and early second centuries the ministerial offices of the local church at Rome had not yet attained the distinction and clarity seen in the letters of Ignatius of Antioch. In other words, the leadership role in the local church of Rome was still being exercised collectively before the emergence of a monarchical bishop in Rome.[29]

Such a view is becoming increasingly widespread. the evidence here, as with most subjects of this period, is fragmentary and the issue can be debated in both ways. But the evidence available seems to point predominantly if not decisively in the direction of a collective leadership. Dogmatic *a priori* theses should not force us into presuming or requiring something that the evidence leans against.

What then is the evidence from those writings or authors known as the Apostolic Fathers? Two are of Roman origin, the *Shepherd* of Hermas and the letter of Clement, and one of non-Roman origin, the letter of Ignatius of Antioch to Rome. Ignatius wrote his letters ostensibly to thank the local communities in Asia Minor for their kind assistance to him as a prisoner for Christ but more precisely to warn them against dangers to unity and, as we have seen, to urge the importance of a single strong authoritative leader of the local community. Throughout these six letters, he broadcasts his theological views of the central importance of the bishop. But he also wrote one letter ahead, to a place which he had never visited personally but where he was to end his life as a martyr— Rome. His purpose here was quite different—to ask the Roman Christians not to interfere on his behalf to try to stop his trial and suffering. The letter is interesting because, unlike all the other letters, it contains no ecclesiological doctrine about the importance of the bishop. Of course, as he himself says, he did not presume to give the Roman Christians instructions as the Apostles had. Nevertheless it is strange that while the other letters all make frequent mention of the bishop of the community being addressed, he does not greet a bishop in Rome nor does he ever mention such a person in this letter. One might object that since Ignatius had never been in Rome, he did not know the bishop's name. He could have spoken to or of a bishop even if he had not known his name. More importantly, if one should presume from his other letters that a strong individual bishop-leader existed everywhere in the Church of his time, then he would have known that there was such a leader in the Roman community. But we have only silence, which leads many to conclude that Ignatius did not address such a person because the Roman community of the time had no such leader.

The two other documents of relevance are of Roman origin themselves. First is the longest and probably the most unusual of the Apostolic Fathers, the *Shepherd* of Hermas. Hermas was a farmer, an ex-slave who was a member of the Roman community who received what we would call visions and private revelations, most of which concern the problem of sin in the Church and the issue of public penance. What is of interest here are the incidental remarks which mention the leaders of the Christian community in Rome. These leaders are usually referred to by such vague titles as "the leaders" (e.g., Vision II.2.6; III.9.7). Sometimes they are called elders as "the elders who are in charge of the Church" (Vis. II.4.3). It is significant to note that these references are all in the plural. In other places, bishops are mentioned (again in the plural); they are usually linked with others, e.g., bishops, teachers and deacons (Vis. III.5.1) in the context of the image of the Church as a tower under construction. The author is describing various types of stones that go into the building of the tower. In this passage, he appears to be speaking about the great figures of the past.

Hermas claimed to be a lay member of the community. On the other hand, Clement is a member of the leadership group, indeed by common traditional estimation, the fourth Pope and the third bishop after Peter. There is further, a considerable body of literature attributed to Clement, all of which except I Clement or the letter of Clement, has been taken from him, so to speak. Ironically, the one item left, this letter (96 A.D.), does not contain his name. The significance of the letter itself will be discussed in the next chapter; our interest at the moment lies in the picture of leadership of the local Roman community that appears in the letter. In general, neither Clement nor anyone else appears in a position anything like that of the bishop as described by Ignatius.

Not surprisingly, given the purpose of the letter (to rebuke the Corinthian Christians for rebelling against their presbyters), there are several references to the leaders of the Church in Corinth, the presbyters. No indication is given of any different leadership pattern in the Roman church itself. The abstract term *episkope* is used in conjunction with the presbyters (44.5). Once again the picture given seems to point to the leadership being exercised by a collectivity. The word *proegoumenoi* is used (1.3; 21.6) but it is not clear whether the leaders referred to are secular or Church leaders.

A new and important study by Peter Lampe draws the picture of the early Roman community divided into a number of smaller house churches scattered throughout the city and its environs, each presided over by a presbyter or perhaps more than one). There was really no united and coordinated Church leadership *ad intra,* i.e., within the city's Christian community as a whole. *Ad extra,* however, with reference to relations with the Christian communities of other cities, there was a united face. One presbyter, e.g., Clement as specifically mentioned in the *Shepherd* of Hermas, was charged with corresponding with other Christian communities and probably with dispensing the apparently not inconsiderable aid sent to communities in need. Clement and other such "foreign ministers" of the Roman Church were not monarchical bishops, but the presbyters holding such a position would necessarily stand out.

This evidence (Clement, Hermas, Ignatius) points us in the direction of assuming that in the first century and into the second, there was no bishop of Rome in the usual sense given to that title. The office of the single *mon-episkopos* was slowly emerging in the local Christian communities around the Mediterranean world. Men like Ignatius were strongly urging this development. But the evidence seems to indicate that in the earliest decades, this evolution had not yet been accomplished in Rome. This then is that missing link referred to by Rudolf Pesch. If there were no bishop of Rome, in what sense can one speak of a Petrine succession?

II

The Church Is in the Bishop[1]

Our topic in this chapter is the early period, that is, not only the second and third centuries, but for the Papacy, even the first two-thirds of the fourth century to a date some fifty years after the victory of Constantine. It is a difficult period to make definitive judgments about because of the lack of documentation. From the time of Pope Damasus (366-384), the evidence for the Roman view of itself become abundant. (See chapter 5.) I might point out that this distinction between what Rome says about itself and what other, non-Roman sources say about Roman authority, is one that must be observed throughout this enquiry. Before the time of Damasus, evidence from both sources is sketchy and sporadic.

Such a state of affairs is obviously not uncommon in the study of ancient history. The question is: What do we make of it? Two extremes are to be avoided. Many Catholics might tend *a priori* for dogmatic reasons to assert that, the Roman primacy being of divine origin, the functioning of the Papacy such as would be seen from 366 on, must be presumed to be the same before that date. Perhaps a great deal of documentation has been lost. Perhaps but not likely. The other extreme would be to claim that the first papal position was the product of a single-minded and determined campaign by a series of Roman bishops from 366 on. Could that position and prestige simply have been created *ex nihilo* in 366? Not likely. There are enough bits of evidence from before the time of Damasus to indicate that the Roman position at least (not

---

* Notes for this chapter can be found on pp. 153-56

necessarily saying anything about the position of non-Romans) was developing through this period of relative silence and quiescence. These quiet years are the focus of this chapter. (The evidence from North Africa will be studied as a whole, both before and after Constantine, in the next chapter).

It must be recognized at the start that within the world-wide Christian Church, the Roman community was viewed with respect and even affection. As Paul had already written in Romans 1.8, "Your faith is proclaimed (*katangelletai*) in all the world." This respect should be kept in mind when sifting the non-Roman evidence. It was due to some extent perhaps to the historical position of Rome itself but much more, I believe, as time went on because this was the see and the resting place of Peter and Paul. Thus when Eastern authors[2] in particular praise St. Peter, the import of this for their view of Rome's authority in the contemporary Church needs to be weighed carefully. Respect and affection do not necessarily mean that the other local churches, especially in the East, accord the Roman church rights of direct command over them.

Bishop-Lists[3]

The first chapter ended somewhat in suspense: Was there a Roman bishop or not in the first and early second centuries? Even if we assume as correct the hypothesis mentioned at the end of the first chapter, namely, that historically there was no monarchical bishop in Rome during that period, it is my own view that such a situation is less troublesome for the history of the Papacy than might appear at first sight.

It has been noted that whatever a given Christian denomination may call the authoritative leaders(s) of its local communities, whatever title they may be given—pastor, superintendent, board of elders, etc.—in fact in every case some individual or group is charged with exercising the task of *episkope*,[4] oversight, literally, or, in general, leadership. Recall the statement made in the letter of Clement (44.1): "Our Apostles knew through our Lord Jesus Christ that there would be strife for the title of bishop" (*episkope*). It may have been that a group known by the general title of elders exercised *episkope* in the Roman community for several decades. Could not the embryonic Papacy have been born from that leadership group?

One further important bit of evidence should be considered in relation to this question. Indeed, this particular issue, the existence of lists of the bishops of the principal sees, might be brought forward as an objection to the hypothesis that Rome once had no monarchical bishop. Although such lists arose at a fairly early date, their genesis is not to be traced to an interest in antiquarian detail for its own sake. Such lists were an important weapon in the growing battle with heresy, above all with Gnosticism. The Gnostics possessed a certain intellectual and spiritual snob appeal, claiming to offer esoteric but salvific knowledge not available to the common human herd, indeed not available to the common flock of Christians. Orthodox apologists like Irenaeus could attack Gnosticism with a good deal of ridicule for its pretensions and often absurd jargon and obscure mythology, as well as for the seemingly infinite divergences and variations among its teachers. Despite all this, it was still perceived as a threat not to be taken lightly.

The Gnostics also claimed to possess the teaching of Christ received through the channels of a secret tradition.[5] (Cf. the letter of Ptolemy to Flora cited in Epiphanius.) This was countered by apologists who emphasized the public nature of the tradition held in the Church. Each local church, especially Rome, founded by Apostles could point to a sort of historical, publicly attested pedigree, its list of its own bishops. In the early fourth century, the pioneer Church historian Eusebius, bishop of Caesarea in Palestine, used these bishop lists of the important sees as one of the pivotal supports for the framework of his history. But that does not mean in his case that all the names are beyond dispute. For example, the tradition that Mark the Evangelist[6] was the founder of the Church in Alexandria is considered quite unhistorical. But the list of the Roman bishops is another question.

Already in the mid-second century, the Jewish-Christian

writer Hegesippus[7] tells us that he travelled the Mediterranean world, visiting the principal churches and found their doctrine, unlike that of the Gnostics, uniform and definite. His works are lost but Eusebius cited him in five places. The most significant of his comments concerns his visit to Rome. "When I came to Rome, I recovered the list of the succession (literally, "I made a succession") until Anicetus, and after him came Eleutherus. In each list and in each city, things are as the Law, the Prophets and the Lord preach" (*H.E.* IV.22). Unfortunately, at this point in Eusebius, the list itself is not given. Rather, the oldest list from c. 180 is that of Irenaeus of Lyons (*Adversus haereses* III.3.3) in a text we shall discuss later. This text of Irenaeus is also cited by Eusebius.

The important point here is: Does such a list of names prove the existence of the monarchical episcopate in Rome all the way back to Peter? After all, there are the names, Linus, Cletus, Clement, etc. Not necessarily. The recent study by Peter Lampe mentioned at the end of the first chapter comments upon the question of the list of the bishops of Rome. He also regards Victor's predecessors after 150 as the presbyters charged with the Roman community's "external relations". Such were Anicetus (155-166) who greeted Polycarp on his visit from Smyrna; Soter (166-174) who wrote to the Corinthians; and Eleutherus (174-189) who dealt with both Irenaeus in Gaul and Montanists in Asia Minor. From the time of Eleutherus comes the list found in Irenaeus. Lampe expresses a certain suspicion that the list, probably furnished Irenaeus by the Roman church, seems artificial. He points out that Eleutherus is the twelfth bishop in the list (Sixtus being the sixth!). The list does not include Peter but seems constructed so as to recapitulate the Twelve Apostles. Irenaeus' list then, concludes Lampe, is a construction of the 180's.

I believe that we have here a reading back into the first century of the role of the community bishop as found in the mid-second century. Is it pure fiction then? No. I do not see why this has to be the case. The collective leadership counted among their number men who stood out from the crowd; people perhaps who frequently exercised a de facto leadership but without being monarchical bishops.

N.B.

Perhaps Linus and Cletus were such. Clement may well have been, given his later reputation. Even in a collective leadership, some officers were known as *episkopoi*. This I think would be sufficient to fulfill the requirement strongly stated by Ignatius of Antioch (*Trall.* 3.1) that "without these (i.e., bishops, presbyters and deacons), the community is not called a church." Christian communities including Rome had such local officers even if one was not yet really like the strong single *episkopos* extolled by Ignatius. Thus while I do not accept bishop lists, even relatively reliable ones such as Rome's, to be proof positive of the existence of the monarchical episcopate in the first century, neither do I see them as baseless inventions of later generations.

The Apostolic Fathers

Two documents from the Apostolic Fathers have already received some attention for the evidence they bring to bear upon the question of the form of government of the local church of Rome. The letter of Clement and the letter of Ignatius of Antioch to Rome are also both brought forward as examples of evidence of Roman authority. Both naturally have been much discussed. Should they be considered as evidence for Roman authority at an early date? The comments of Ignatius are proof of what we have already mentioned, namely, the respect in which the Roman church was held. The question of the exercise of Roman authority arises with the letter of Clement.

Ignatius of Antioch

Ignatius of Antioch wrote one letter ahead to Rome to ask that Christians there do nothing that might impede his martyrdom. The precise text in question here is the opening greeting of that letter. It is longer and more ornate than the greetings which preface his other letters. Within this section, two phrases in particular have drawn the attention of commentators: (The Church) "which presides in the country of the land of the Romans." This is taken to mean no more than that the local church of Rome is the principal church in the environs of Rome or perhaps in central Italy. More importantly, there is this comment: (the Roman church) "pre-eminent in love" (*agape*).[8] A Catholic scholar like Johannes Quasten has interpreted *agape* here as the equivalent of the Catholic Church— thus the local church of Rome presides over the universal Catholic Church. This view has not attracted many adherents. Of the other views suggested, I find Harnack's the most likely. He suggested that the local church of Rome was already outstanding in the world for its practical charity. Several instances are cited in Eusebius. In the late second century (c. 170), Dionysius of Corinth wrote to Soter of Rome: "This has been your custom from the beginning, to do good in manifold ways to all Christians and to send contributions to the many Churches in every city, in some places relieving the poverty of the needy and ministering to the Christians in the mines by the contribution which you have sent from the beginning, preserving the ancestral custom of the Romans, true Romans as you are" (*H.E.* IV.23). About 256, Dionysius of Alexandria wrote to Pope Stephen concerning the situation of the Church in Syria and Arabia "which you constantly help and to which you have now written..." (*H.E.* VII.5). Later in the fourth century, Basil of Caesarea spoke of how in the previous century, Dionysius of Rome had written to his own church in Cappadocia (Basil, *ep.* 70). The Roman see then was outstanding in its charitable consideration for even distant parts of the Church.

Clement of Rome[9]

Such concern was not limited to material aid as the letter of Clement shows. This letter is usually dated about fifteen or twenty years before that of Ignatius, i.e., *circa* 96 A.D. For all that has been said or written about Clement, in fact we know little about him. He is the Clement of the *Clementine Homilies and Recognitions,* the principal works of the so-called pseudo-Clementine literature. According to a tradition known to

Tertullian, he was ordained a bishop by Peter himself,[10] though this brings about a new problem—what to do with Linus and Cletus, names which precede Clement's in the traditional bishop-list of Rome. In the *Shepherd of Hermas,* a Clement is mentioned to whom Hermas is to give the text of his revelations. This makes him seem like the elder in charge of dealing with other communities: "Clement shall send it to the cities abroad for that is his duty" (Vis. II.4.3). All this presumes that we are speaking of one and the same person. This in fact is generally presumed, although Clement was a common name.

Ironically, in this letter, the one writing still attributed to him, Clement's name does not appear. The letter is ostensibly from the Roman community (rather than from an individual, though communities do not write letters) to the Christian community of Corinth which had been having internal difficulties. In Corinth the presbyters, for reasons unknown, had been deposed. Rome, on the contrary, using scriptural examples, urged the need for good order in the Church, (e.g., 37; 40) and the blessings of Church unity (46). The letter contains many details of both value and great significance for the future. The martyrdom of Peter and Paul in Rome is cited as a latter-day example of the evil fruits of dissension. Though as discussed earlier, collective leadership rather than the monarchical episcopate still seems to be the rule in Rome and Corinth, the all-important basic principle of apostolic succession is stated in chapter 42. God sent Christ who in turn sent the Apostles to preach. And then they appointed " . . . their first converts . . . to be bishops and deacons of the future believers" (42.4). And this principle in turn should ensure that the leaders of the community, even if elected by the faithful, are not thereby simply removable by the community. Because of this link with the Apostles and with Christ, those who lead the community come to have a higher legitimation. To be sure, he adds that the Corinthian presbyters " . . . have ministered . . . without blame, humbly, peaceably and disinterestedly and for many years have received a universally favorable testimony" (44).

The principle of apostolic succession is of basic importance, though it is applied here to the elders rather than to a single bishop. Our question is one which has been asked for centuries:

Is this letter to be understood as an exercise of the Roman primacy? Consider that Corinth was itself a significant Christian community of Apostolic foundation. (I Cor 1.12: Peter and Paul!) Further, if tradition is correct, though Peter and Paul were long dead, there was still one of the original Twelve alive, John in Ephesus or on Patmos, both considerably closer to Corinth than Rome. The letter begins with something of a Roman apology for the delay in getting to their problem (1). All of this seems to point to a sense of Roman obligation for the welfare of other communities, even those well removed geographically.

And so Catholic scholars have frequently claimed for this letter the honor of being the first exercise of Roman primacy. Opponents have seen it simply as an example of fraternal correction such as might be carried on between two equal local churches at that time. Was one local church at this time considered superior in rank to other local churches? If the Roman self-consciousness of its own superior position was a fact at this time, why does this exercise of such authority appear to be so isolated? Were there more such interventions but the records are lost?

Or does it all come down to opinions about the tone of the letter? Is it a tone of command? of superiority? How is one to measure such things? Exhortation to obedience and warnings are found at the end of the letter. The Corinthians are to be obedient to God; the letter is referred to as *symboule,* "counsel" (58). On the other hand, if the "tone" is claimed to be simply one of fraternal correction, are there other such letters? The answer is yes. Eusebius speaks of Bishop Dionysius of Corinth who, apparently unsolicited, wrote letters of advice and exhortation to many churches such as the Athenians and Nicomedians (*H.E.* IV.23). Thus the question of how to evaluate the Roman intervention is less simple than it may appear, especially recalling the natural prestige of the Roman community suggested earlier.

Travellers to Rome

There is another fact involving Roman prestige the import

of which is difficult to interpret. Eusebius mentions that in the second and early third centuries, many Christian notables, not least a number of heretical leaders, paid visits to Rome or came to stay. Within the context of this enquiry, what is one to make of this? That Roman prestige alone was good enough reason for such a visit is shown from the account of the visit of the third century Alexandrian theologian Origen who desired "to see the most ancient church of the Romans" (*H.E.* VI.15.10). Others, like Justin came from Samaria to settle in Rome where he set up his own private school for instruction in Christian philosophy. One of his students, Tatian, went back to the East where he became a leading exponent of exaggerated asceticism. Irenaeus, on the other hand, visited Rome after emigrating from Smyrna in Asia Minor to Lyons. Some think that he may also have been a student of Justin.

Several prominent Gnostic teachers also visited Rome, the most noted of whom, Marcion from Sinope on the southern shore of the Black Sea, became a member of the Roman community for a while until his views became better known and he was expelled together with the generous financial contribution he had made upon entering. More names could be given but our question is: why? Why did these people, fairly numerous and prominent, come to Rome? Origen's stated purpose may be accepted as sufficient reason: to see, to hear, to join, perhaps to persuade of the truth of one's own views, "the most ancient church of the Romans." Roman prestige and centrality are sufficient reason for this phenomenon.

Irenaeus of Lugdunum

Irenaeus stands out in the battle against Gnosticism. His *Adversus haereses* gives many details about such beliefs but, beyond information, he also develops the counter-argument on the basis of tradition and authority. The community leaders are the ones who have been entrusted with the primary responsibility for the defense of the Gospel against heresy and the preservation of the apostolic tradition. Hegesippus claimed to have verified personally the uniformity of the teaching found in the principal churches of the Mediterranean world. The historical guarantee of such continuity was the list of the bishops of these same sees.

Irenaeus' climactic argument,[11] found in book three, points out that while the testing and verification process can be done with any of the apostolically founded churches, it would take too much time and space to list all the bishops of all these churches. Thus, for the sake of brevity, Irenaeus confines himself to speaking of "the very great, the very ancient and universally known church founded and organized at Rome by the two most glorious Apostles, Peter and Paul" (III.3.2). The text which follows is one of the most frequently discussed testimonies to Roman primacy. An additional reason for dispute is philological. While the text was written in Greek, only a very literal Latin translation remains. Here is the text in question: "... for with this church, by reason of its more excellent origin (*potior principalitas*) every church must agree, i.e., the faithful from everywhere—the church in which always, to the benefit of these people from all over, the tradition which comes from the Apostles has been preserved."

The essential point is made in the first half of the quotation, namely, the Roman church stands out above all others because of Peter and Paul, its two founding apostles. All churches must agree with it on matters of doctrine because they must agree with the apostolic tradition preserved by the apostolic churches. The second half of this translation is probably essentially correct though the Latin is more muddled here than in the first part, enabling scholars to dispute precisely who it is who is supposed to preserve the tradition from the apostles. In any event this is a striking testimony though not, in my view, as decisive as some have urged. The context of Irenaeus' argument does not claim that the Roman church is literally unique, the one and only in its class; rather, he argues that the Roman church is the outstanding example of its class, the class in question being apostolic sees. While he chose to speak primarily of Rome for brevity's sake, in fact, before finishing, he also referred to Ephesus and Smyrna.

Rome was the only see of its kind in the West where he now lived and preached. The argument apparently makes Rome the outstanding example for the Church throughout the entire world. The German Catholic scholar, Norbert Brox of Regensburg, has claimed that the argument is framed entirely within a western context. At first I found this argument weak, but after comparing Irenaeus' argument to its expansion as found in Tertullian's *De praescriptione haereticorum* (36), (cf. next chapter), I find Brox's argument more convincing.

The Quartodeciman Controversy

In this early period, of necessity, we are dealing with a scattering of evidence. One somewhat clouded but significant incident is known as the Quartodeciman controversy. Then as now, Christians in different parts of the world celebrated the Lord's crucifixion and resurrection on different dates. At this time the question was not simply one of varying methods for calculating the date of the feasts. Some Christians in Asia Minor, on its western coast, celebrated the Lord's suffering and glorification on the fourteenth day of the Jewish month of Nisan, whichever day of the week that happened to fall on in a given year. (Hence the name "quartodeciman" = 14). On this day the fast was also to end. This issue had been a sore point for some time. One of the early visitors to Rome was Polycarp, the elderly, respected leader of the Christians of Smyrna who made the long trip to Rome to discuss the issue with bishop Anicetus,[12] shortly after the middle of the second century. They could agree only to disagree but this did not bring about a break. Anicetus parted with Polycarp in respect and Christian love.

Anicetus' more authoritarian successor, Victor, was not so tolerant of variations at the end of the century. The fifth book of Eusebius' *Church History* gives the account. Councils were held throughout the world on the issue, agreeing that the Lord's resurrection should be celebrated only on Sunday. The bishops of Asia, however, refused to change their practice. Their leader, Polycrates of Ephesus, wrote to bishop Victor to explain that their tradition was of long standing, supported by many great men of the past and, thus, they would not yield.

In his letter, Polycrates revealed that it was Rome which had requested (required?) the series of regional councils. These meetings took aim at the practice of the Asians who nevertheless refused to renounce their traditions. As Polycrates insisted, they were "not afraid of threats." Whose threats? That question is quickly answered by Eusebius who informs us that Victor's reply to Polycrates was swift and decisive: "Upon this, Victor ... immediately tried to cut off from the common unity the dioceses of all Asia, together with the adjacent churches, on the ground of heterodoxy..." (*H.E.* V.24.9). He went on to share that while the rest of the Church disagreed with the Asian practices, they thought that Victor overreacted. Irenaeus in particular, who had come from Smyrna himself, asked why the churches could not go on living together in harmony as they had up to now. "... Disagreement in the fast confirms our agreement in the faith" (*H.E.* V.24.13). But Roman views on unity already included uniformity of practice as well as of faith.

The incident shows considerable authority of leadership in the Roman Church at the end of the second century. Some scholars[13] have sought to portray this controversy in quite a different perspective. They maintain that Eusebius, writing more than a century after the events, cast the controversy in an anachronistic light, portraying Roman authority, for example, as it appeared in the fourth century rather than as it was at the end of the second century. These scholars further maintain that Eusebius blew out of proportion what was really simply a dispute *within* the local church at Rome and transformed it into an international contest of wills.

At first sight, these suggestions seem to have some plausibility. As Giorgio LaPiana[14] has argued, the Roman church in the second century was not nearly so uniform as one might think. On the contrary, there were many immigrants in Rome and the Christians among them not surprisingly tended to seek out their co-religionists from their own areas (national parishes?). Furthermore, Ps. Tertullian's treatise *Against all Heresies* mentions a Roman presbyter named Blastus "who would latently introduce Judaism. For he says the Passion is not to be kept otherwise than according to the Law of Moses, on the fourteenth day of the month" (8). Thus in reality, they argue, bishop Victor was simply trying to bring about greater unity among Christians in Rome by forcing communities to abandon their peculiarities in favor of greater uniformity.

In my own view, this explanation has merit in giving a possible or even probable scenario for the origins of the controversy. When the local Quartodeciman community in Rome was criticized, it appealed for support to the church "back home"—hence Polycarp's visit. but I do not believe that the controversy remained restricted to Rome. It spread, and the convoking of a series of regional councils to try to pressure the Asians into conformity is a tribute to Roman prestige. However, the question of the effectiveness of Roman authority is another question. The rest of the Church already agreed with the Roman practice. Despite the pressure exerted on them, the Asians, as far as we know, did not at that moment abandon their traditional views and practices. The issue in fact was a deeper one than perceived at the time, namely, could their be long held traditions in different parts of the Church that differed? Did the Church of Rome recognize such a possibility? Was it wise to use its prestige in such an enterprise?

The Alexandrians

Earlier we mentioned in passing how Origen of Alexandria[15] had visited Rome (c.211-217), where he heard the leading Roman presbyter, Hippolytus, preach. Clement, on the other hand, never made such a trip to our knowledge. Earlier he had been attracted from Athens to Alexandria. His theology of the Church and Origen's as well are harder to detect because they are usually wrapped in a heavy veil of allegorical exegesis, especially of the Old Testament. The fact that Origen does not speak of Roman authority does not prove much since he rarely speaks of Church structures. He is interested in the role of the spiritual men in the Church. "Every imitator of Christ is a rock ... And upon every such rock is built every word of the Church ... for whosoever is perfect, in him is the Church that God is building" (*Comm. in Matt.* XII.10).

So every holy man is a Peter, a rock of the Church. He

alludes to people who believe that the Church is built on Peter alone and asks: "Is it not also built on John?" (XI.11). Is this to be understood as evidence that Origen knew of those who claimed that the Church was built on Peter and that this was related to a Roman primacy? Was he polemicizing against those who attributed such a role to Peter in the Church? Perhaps, but this must remain speculation. At least it is clear that such a plain recognition of Roman primacy or of a connection between Peter and the contemporary bishop of Rome seems remote from Origen's thoughts.

A great deal of the period between 260 and 300 A.D. seems notable for its lack of documentation about anything to do with the Church, a black hole that has never been satisfactorily explained. One brief flash of illumination from c.260 shows us an exchange between the bishops of Rome and Alexandria, both of whom are named Dionysius. The exchange of letters concerned the difficult question of the Trinity, which was far from definitively concluded. It was difficult to maintain the thin line of orthodoxy between Modalism on the one hand and Tritheism or Subordinationism on the other. Misunderstandings had their part in this exchange. Rome seemed to take a position of supervision vis-a-vis Alexandria. This exchange likewise laid the foundation of, or at least gives an early example of, the special relationship between Rome and Alexandria. Alexandria, the second see, the see of Mark the Evangelist, disciple of Peter, is subject only to the first see, the see of Peter.

Here I must confess to wicked thoughts. This exchange is known because Athanasius has preserved this text. And he preserved it because it supports his case against the Arians from two points of view. First, Dionysius is represented as teaching that the Son is begotten but not made. The Son is not a creature and he even specifically refutes the favorite Arian scriptural text, Prov. 8.22. Second, as Athanasius was supported by Rome in his serious battle against his Eastern detractors, he is happy to stress the contacts of one of his predecessors with the Roman bishop. All of this seems too convenient but, to my knowledge, no one has called into question the authenticity of the fragments.

Charges of Heresy against Roman Bishops

Before proceeding to the time of Constantine, the issue of Roman orthodoxy should be mentioned. In 1870, three great matters were brought forward as serious historical objections to papal infallibility. These were the cases of Pope Liberius in the fourth century; Vigilius in the sixth and Honorius in the seventh. We shall later see something of the first two cases, both of which are clearly cases involving coercion. The Honorius case seems to be a more obvious instance of failure of the papal charism of *vigilantia*. But some earlier accusations of Roman indiscretion often seem to be ignored.

In one of these instances, Tertullian intimated that a bishop of Rome (Victor?) was inclined "to recognize the prophecies of Montanus (*Adversus Praxean* 1). What does this mean? Some have even suggested that the bishop of Rome was going to become a Montanist or at least that he was leaning toward approval of this controversial group. Tertullian's report emphasizes that a dubious character and heretic named Praxeas dissuaded the bishop from such a move. Robin Lane Fox's recent suggestion[16] that this is the first case of an appeal to Rome (by Montanus!) requires the acceptance of several related but unproved hypotheses. We know so little about this incident that it would be going too far to see this as a close-run thing—of a near Roman approval of Montanus. That would be rather unlikely. What it does show is that in Tertullian's view, such an approval would be a significant move against Montanus' episcopal enemies in Asia Minor. Of course, Tertullian's statement seems to claim that not only did Praxeas succeed in turning the bishop away from Montanism but toward Patripassianism as well, a form of Trinitarian modalist heresy. More significant is the declaration that Praxeas succeeded in this "by insistence on the decisions of the bishop's predecessors" (*Idem*). How often in history since have Popes, whatever their own inclination in a given matter, felt bound by the decisions of their predecessors? (e.g., *Humanae vitae* of 1968).

Hippolytus

The noteworthy Roman presbyter and theologian Hippolytus also had charges of his own to register. In a city and church not noted as a center for creative theology, Hippolytus stands out as an unimaginative but still significant author. Even today an ancient statue of him, unearthed during the Renaissance, can be found at the foot of the staircase at the entrance of the Vatican Library. Since he wrote in Greek, it has been disputed whether he was a native Roman or not. His *Apostolic Tradition*[17] is perhaps the single most precious document for the study of the early liturgy. Much of his other work is slower going. He is also the source of our knowledge of Roman ecclesiastical history of the early third century. Source? Yes, but a very distorted one for his is the voice of the scorned and disappointed office-seeker. Having failed to become bishop legitimately, he broke away to be the first important anti-pope or schismatic bishop in papal history.

His particular claim was that he maintained the earlier rigoristic purity of the Church over against (as he saw it) the growing laxity of penitential practice. His descriptions of his successful rival Callistus are a caricature and almost funny. He depicts him, an ex-slave and accused embezzler, continually duping the well-meaning but ineffectual bishop Zephyrinus, "an uneducated simpleton". He accused Zephyrinus of ignorance and Callistus of shameless opportunism in matters of doctrine as well. In one instance, he claimed that after he (Hippolytus) had converted Sabellius to the orthodox view, Callistus permitted or persuaded him to relapse.

This was all being said for Church-political reasons but, nevertheless, Callistus was being accused of promoting unorthodoxy. He was even accused of promoting abortion. He supported orthodoxy only when it suited his political aims. "A senseless and unstable fellow, who improvises blasphemies in every direction . . . He is not abashed at leaning now toward the doctrine of Sabellius, now towards that of Theodotus" (Hippolytus. *Refutation of All Heresies* IX.12.19).[18] Such accusations of unorthodoxy against a bishop of Rome have not drawn all that much attention during the battle over infallibility, partially because of the obvious bias of Hippolytus and partly because of the intrinsic difficulty of dealing with the Trinitarian questions which at this point in their evolution had by no means reached maturity.

So while Hippolytus protests against this or that aspect of Callistus' views, from the point of view of later dogmatic decisions, Hippolytus' own views are by no means unobjectionable. Finally, we may note that a generation after Hippolytus, there was yet another Roman schism, led by another theologian, Novatian(us), the first Roman theologian to write in Latin. This schism too brings charges of official Roman laxity and excessive leniency in dealing with those who had fallen or apostatized during the mid-third century persecution of Decius. It is of less theological significance than the protest of Hippolytus.

Final Persecution and Triumph

The terrible ordeal of the Roman empire in the third century came to end when one of the soldier emperors, Diocletian, the only one of the many who tried, succeeded in his efforts at stabilization of the situation. The new empire of Diocletian, the *Dominate* as historians call it, is usually pictured as the Roman empire restored to order because it was placed under martial law, in effect in a straight-jacket of raw authoritarianism greater than anything hitherto experienced. Scholars have debated the accuracy of such a depiction as well as the factual effectiveness of certain measures which threatened to put society into a sort of deep-freeze or into an intellectual and financial suit of armor.

We need not go into such details here. Suffice it to say that Constantine[19] enters our history because he was the son of the junior emperor of the West in Diocletian's tetrarchy, Constantius Chlorus. Starting from York where he had been acclaimed Augustus by his father's troops after his father's death in 306, he marched to the gates of Rome where the climactic battle of the Milvian Bridge in the northern suburbs of Rome took place in 312. His opponent, Maxentius, was also technically a usurper, though, like Constantine, the son of a former tetrarch. Maxentius had already proclaimed toleration for Christians. Perhaps the major difference between the two was that now Constantine was to proclaim himself a Christian.

Constantine's conversion has been a constant subject of debate among historians. Was it genuine? Was it a calculated political move? Today most would consider it a genuine conversion but according to his own lights. For centuries Roman rulers, including those who had most fervently persecuted the Christians, believed that the gods would bless the world, the empire and the rulers themselves provided they were worshipped correctly as they demanded. Roman religion had a large component of the *quid pro quo,* the *do ut des* about it.[20]

Constantine too worshipped the new God who had brought him victory over his enemies. He also began to shower gifts upon Christians, property, money, privileges for the clergy, both in Rome and elsewhere.[21] The new basilicas he began to build in Rome on the reputed sites of the deaths of the founder-Apostles, Peter and Paul, brought new prestige to the Roman church beyond what it had previously known. These new Christian monuments rose on the periphery of the ancient city, embodying in a striking way the Christian role as newcomers and upstarts.

Many medieval legends rose around the interaction of Constantine and Bishop Sylvester of Rome.[22] Indeed, Sylvester later became a leading villain in the sectarian scenario which pictured the downfall of the Church brought about by the corruption of the Church now showered with riches by a well-meaning emperor. Another legend has Constantine as a leper warned in a dream to search for Sylvester. He found him, and his leprosy was cured when he was baptized by the Pope. All of these are nonsense. Sylvester was not even bishop when Constantine overthrew Maxentius at the Milvian Bridge. Miltiades was. Nor was Constantine baptized in Rome; he was baptized in the East in his palace in Nicomedia as he lay dying in 337 and by an Arian bishop at that, Eusebius of Nicomedia.

After he became sole emperor in 324, he founded his capital, New Rome, the city of Constantine. This move to the East also gave rise to the even more momentous forgery, the Donation of Constantine, by which the emperor, abandoning Rome and the West for the East, had turned everything in the West over to the bishop of Rome. It is amazing then how much legend accumulated around Constantine and the bishop of Rome and how little of it had any basis.

Constantine[23] once described himself, according to his friend, the great historian, bishop Eusebius of Caesarea in Palestine, as the *episkopos ton ektos,* the bishop of those outside, while the Church bishops were the bishops of those inside. But in fact Constantine felt a special obligation to oversee the welfare of the Church, as Eusebius put it: "He watched over all his subjects with an episcopal care. . ." (*Vita Constantini* IV.24). He, wishing to have God smile on him as well as on Church and empire, in fact acted as if he were entrusted with the *episkope,* oversight of the whole Church. Unlike his son, Constantius II, he did not see it as his duty to dictate doctrine to the Church. When he became emperor in the West in 312, he found the Donatist schism in North Africa; when he took power in the East in 324, the more serious Arian problem was already raging there. In either case, he concentrated his efforts in trying to help the Church put its own house in order by facilitating the gathering of large numbers of bishops in councils (Arles, 314; Nicaea, 325). When their decisions had been made, the government would back them in terms of civil law, outlawing both dissent and, if necessary, the dissenters. In addition, as we have seen, money, property and privileges all flowed to the Church. So, in a noteworthy way, Constantine was exercising a certain type of leadership for the entire Church while the role of the bishops of Rome on the same world stage remained relatively obscure and undetermined.

The role of the bishops of Rome in the great Christological councils of the fifth century is an important one that will be detailed in chapters five and six. But such is not the case for the council of Nicaea. The first great ecumenical council was summoned by the emperor.[24] The bishop of Rome, indeed the western bishops in general, had a negligible role. Two priests represented the see of Rome but signed the decrees after the presiding bishop, Ossius of Cordoba,[25] a see of no great importance in a remote province of Spain. We do not know how Ossius came to know Constantine, but he came to be an ecclesiastical advisor to the emperor, one of his intimates, who exercised apparently a greater role in the Church of the time than did Sylvester.

As noted earlier, Rome for all its importance in other ways was not a theological center in the ancient Church. This is true of the West in general, with the possible exception of North Africa. Of all the great western Fathers, the sole creative theologian of world significance was Augustine. The Greek East was the center of creative thinking. Its active bishops like Athanasius, Basil, the Gregories, Cyril of Alexandria were also original theologians. In a world where tradition is a primary value, creativity has its risks. As Jerome put it: it takes brains to be a heretic. Not that the West was devoid of brains, but it was the Greek world with its philosophical heritage that attempted to tackle the complex questions of the Trinity and Christology. How are the persons related in the Trinity? Are they equal or subordinate? How is the human related to the divine in Jesus? Is he fully divine and fully human? *Hypostasis, ousia,* and other similar technical terms obviously all come from the East. Rome and the West usually simply reacted positively or negatively to Eastern developments.

If Rome had little or nothing to do with the fashioning of the *homoousios* of Nicaea, it did stand steadfastly against the sustained campaign against Nicaea and against the man who came practically to be its embodiment, Athanasius,[26] bishop of Alexandria from 328-373 (with five periods of exile interspersed, two in the West). Unfortunately, for this period, the forty years following the council of Nicaea, documents concerning the bishops of Rome are still sketchy. Roman letters which will furnish the bulk of evidence from Damasus on, are still lacking. Within these limits, Pope Julius[27] (337-352) stands out for his unswerving defense of Athanasius and other Eastern exiles, victims of the Eusebians as they were called and of the general campaign against the supporters of Nicaea.

Athanasius had left Alexandria for the second time in 339 because of the continuing pressure against him. He sought refuge in Rome. His Eastern antagonists, apparently thinking that they could now deliver the coup de grace, made the error (according to Athanasius' *Apologia contra Arianos* 20) of inviting Pope Julius to call a council himself. They presumed that the Westerner would join them in their condemnation of Athanasius, and then he would have no place left to hide. But they were wrong. When they realized they had misread the situation, they suddenly did an about face and repudiated the Western call for a council. They asked what right the Western bishops had to interfere in Eastern affairs. Western bishops had no more right to overturn the decisions of Eastern councils than the Eastern bishops had the right to reconsider Western decisions. Julius' reply is a masterpiece of reason and calm rebuke. "I . . . was surprised that, whereas we had written to you in love and sincerity of truth, you should answer us in so hostile and unsuitable a manner. For the pride and arrogance of the writer were conspicuous throughout this writing" (in Athanasius, *Idem,* 21).

Since East and West seemed at an impasse, the two surviving sons of Constantine, Constantius I, Eastern emperor and adversary of Athanasius, and Constans, emperor of the West, proposed a joint council to be held at Sardica[28] (modern Sofia, Bulgaria) in the hope of reuniting the warring factions. The council, meeting *circa* 343, completely failed in that purpose but the Western bishops who remained, with their guests like Athanasius, created at Ossius' suggestion canons which mark a significant milestone in the rise of the Papacy—or at least so it seems in historical retrospect.

In effect, these canons give the Roman see the right to act as a court of appeal, to review the decisions of certain local or regional councils and to make the decision that the case should or should not be heard again. It was not a question of holding a new trial in Rome. Conditions of transportation at that time made that impractical, although in some cases a Roman representative might be sent to take part in the new deliberations. I have made the comment that these canons seem important to us in historical retrospect because it is not clear from the evidence that the Church at that time saw them as equally momentous or, in certain cases, even remembered them at all!

Despite Sardica, the East-West impasse continued until the death of Constans in 350. This meant that Constantius as sole surviving son of Constantine now became sole emperor. And this was very menacing for the Western Church. Constantius[29] now demanded the same submission from the Western bishops he was accustomed to receive in the East. While most Western bishops did not know a *homoousios* from an *hypostasis,* there were certain Western stalwarts who, even if they did not grasp all the theological nuances or have a good knowledge of Greek, nevertheless knew that they must stand with Athanasius at all costs. Hilary of Poitiers, Eusebius of Vercelli, Paulinus of Trier, Lucifer of Cagliari, all stand out as brave men who resisted the emperor to the face and suffered exile for their opposition.

At first, Liberius of Rome[30] was among their number. He rejected bribes and threats until he too was exiled but, unlike those mentioned above, he eventually capitulated. Personally I have never had a great problem with this since his actions were the result of coercion and therefore were of doubtful validity. Further it is not certain which creed or creeds he was forced to adhere to. And there were many such creeds. Relatively few of these explicitly rejected Nicaea and the *homoousios;* most were acceptable in the abstract in what they said explicitly. In practice they were not acceptable because they conspicuously ignored Nicaea. Liberius was allowed to return to Rome where he seems to have suffered little loss of prestige among local Christians, although he was also very silent for the rest of his life. Felix, who had been ordained bishop when Liberius was exiled, was still present and the factions forming behind the two men promised trouble for the future. This trouble would become shockingly apparent in the election of Liberius' successor in 366. We are on the eve of the great blossoming of the papacy which we shall explore in chapter five.

III

The Africans and
Rome across the Sea

The study of North African Christianity[1] reminds us that the Roman world was very much a Mediterranean world, one that encompassed both sides of the interior sea so that it could truly be called *Mare nostrum*. We are used to thinking of the Mediterranean world as split between Christian North and Muslim South. It was all one then. It is this area, what is now Algeria and Tunisia, especially the area around Tunis or Carthage, that was in a very real sense, the birthplace of Latin Christianity, not Italy, Gaul or Spain. This area merits study as a unity for several reasons: its importance to the origins and development of the Western Church and its theology; its regional unity; the specifically ecclesiological interests of its theological writers; its traditional concern for unity with Rome combined with a significant desire for the autonomy of the local church. Going back in time to c. 200, we come to the heyday of the first great Christian writer in Latin.

Tertullian[2] was converted to Christianity c. 194. He is among the most fascinating of authors, always doing battle. His arguments may frequently be sophistical, but they are rarely dull. The great champion of orthodoxy in his early days, he became a Montanist later. Always a rigorist, he wanted more. According to one tradition, even the Montanists proved too tame for him so he went off to form his own group. There is a good deal of irony here as well as sadness since in his orthodox days, he had authored one of the most incisive tracts against

* Notes for this chapter can be found on pp. 156-59

heresy in general, the *De praescriptione haereticorum*.[3] He derives his basic argument from Irenaeus but since he is a more effective writer, the work is more concise and the argument clearer.

Here, as in Irenaeus, the Gnostics, especially Marcion, are the adversaries. If anyone, he argues, of the disciples of Jesus knew the whole of his teachings, the fullness of the truth, it must have been the Twelve. They founded churches around the Mediterranean, especially in the East. It is to these churches that the inquirer should go to find out what Jesus taught, not to the bevy of contradictory Gnostic masters. The particular pedigree of each church is to be found in its list of bishops going back to the founding Apostle. Every church, to be sure, can be an apostolic church doctrinally, if not historically, by teaching what the Apostles taught (*consanguinitas doctrinae*). For those who live in the East, there is always an apostolic church in your vicinity. For Africa the point of reference is the Roman church. And here he adds a brief panegyric: "What a happy church it is, on which the apostles poured out their whole doctrine with their blood; where Peter suffered like his Lord, where Paul was crowned with John's death, where the Apostle John after he had been immersed in boiling oil without harm, was banished to an island" (36). This last mentioned incident seems to be an attempt to explain why John died as an old man whereas it was more fitting that all the Twelve die as martyrs. John tried at least!

Despite this valuable treatise, Tertullian has little to say about the position of Rome. Yes, here and there one finds references to Peter baptizing in the Tiber (*Bapt.* 4) or the Church receiving the keys through Peter (*Scorp.* 10). But what is of some note comes from late in his life during his Montanist period when his rigorism had gotten the better of him. In the *De pudicitia*,[4] he stresses that the most serious sins, murder, adultery and idolatry, are not forgivable sins, at least not forgivable by the Church in this life. Later he specifies that holy men, the spiritual ones who can forgive sins, will not do so. The occasion for this work is the declaration by a bishop that he is willing to forgive sins of adultery. Such a proclamation sent Tertullian into a rage. He mocked this *pontifex maximus*[5] who thought he was an *episcopus episcoporum*. Many have seen the presumptuous prelate as a bishop of Rome, perhaps Callistus embroiled in his argument with Hippolytus. In recent years it has become more common to look upon Tertullian's target as a local Catholic bishop, probably the bishop of Carthage. Terms like *pontifex maximus* were not yet papal or even Christian titles. This and the other title are being used sarcastically by Tertullian. He is asking: Who do you think you are? The repudiation of the title "bishop of bishops" at least highlights a certain African sensitivity to one prelate's claiming authority over other bishops. Cyprian used the title sarcastically also but clearly in an anti-Roman context. Concerning the power of the keys he argues, to suit his purpose, that the power was given to Peter personally, not to other bishops and not to any episcopal successor to Peter.

Cyprian

Unlike Tertullian, Cyprian[6] was a bishop and a martyr; bishop of Carthage, leader of the Church in North Africa. He had been converted to Christianity as a mature man c. 246 and had quickly risen to the top, not without considerable resentment on the part of some of the clergy. He was almost immediately tested with the outbreak of the Decian persecution in 250. This was really the first great persecution of the whole Church decreed by the central authority of the empire as contrasted with earlier sporadic and localized outbreaks. Cyprian himself opted to go into hiding. this was a perfectly acceptable alternative for the laity, but since he was the leader, his actions caused many raised eyebrows. He said that he did it so that the community would not be deprived of pastoral direction. At times in the future, after the end of the persecution, he appeared to be on the defensive about this earlier decision.

There is no debate, however, on what happened to a great many of the Christians. While some died as martyrs rather than sacrifice and others suffered imprisonment, torture, the confiscation of their property, a great many, perhaps the majority, capitulated or lapsed all too easily. Cyprian himself later described the fiasco in his *De lapsis.*[7] Even before the end of the persecution, Cyprian was faced with the problem of what to do with these *lapsi,* numerous as they were. When the persecution was over, very many demanded a rapid and painless re-admission to the Church. Cyprian eventually came to agree that all the lapsed could be re-admitted, provided that they all did public penance. The bishop would hear each case individually and make a decision about the extent of guilt. The nature and the duration of the penance would be specified according to the guilt. After all, there were varying degrees of guilt. Some people had actually sacrificed whereas others had been able to bribe officials to give them a *libellus,* a certificate which testified that they had sacrificed whereas in reality they had not. There were people who had succumbed after terrible tortures while others had flocked to sacrifice without even a pretense of resistance. Cyprian's solution seemed equitable enough, given the rigoristic practice of the day.

But in the event things were not to be so simple. There were some who were in favor of re-admitting almost everyone without further ado; indeed some had already been allowed back into communion. Others, some of Tertullian's stripe, were in favor of going on without such weak Christians as befits a Church for saints only. A further serious complication arose from the practice of some of the confessors—those who had been imprisoned and tortured for the faith but who had not died. There was a long-standing tradition, attested by Tertullian, that martyrs were very special people in the eyes of God. They were charismatic; they had special privileges.

With the growth of the Church and the strengthening of the authority of Church leaders, some of that feeling was dying out. The lapsed thus might go to these confessors for the forgiveness of their sins. Some confessors gave out *libelli pacis,* certificates of peace. Cyprian did not object to this but he did complain when some confessors apparently started handing out such certificates wholesale or wrote them in such a way that they seemed to order the bishop to accept the bearer without further penance as opposed to recommending a person to the bishop's mercy. Here the charismatic clashed with the institutional. Cyprian was the man in charge and he was not going to allow himself to be ordered around. But lest the charismatic-institutional contrast be exaggerated, it should be recalled that Cyprian had something of the charismatic in him, receiving messages from God in dreams.

Cornelius versus Novatian

The persecution in Rome had been equally devastating. Bishop Fabian had been among the first to die, and the situation had been so perilous that the community had been unable to elect a new bishop for some fourteen months. In the interim, a committee of presbyters led by the theologian Novatian,[8] tried to hold things together. One of the early letters in the Cyprianic corpus was written by this group to the Christians of Carthage. The implication of this letter (8) is that while Rome had had a good bishop who had not hesitated to shed his blood for Christ, the Carthaginians were to be consoled because their bishop had shown himself a hireling by abandoning his flock to go into hiding. When Cyprian became aware of this letter, he immediately felt the need to defend his actions. Thus began a noteworthy exchange of letters between Cyprian and Rome. Soon Cyprian's position was understood in Rome and a common policy was agreed upon on how to deal with the lapsed in both churches.

When the persecution had ended and order had been restored, an election was held in the Roman community and the favorite, Novatian, was not chosen. Rather Cornelius became bishop of Rome. There was some initial confusion in Africa, but soon enough Cornelius was recognized and a happy partnership established between the bishops of the two most important sees in the West. They agreed on the middle of the road policy toward the lapsed while Novatian, claiming, like Hippolytus a generation earlier, to be the champion of the old-time rigorism, found himself speedily excluded from the flock and the new anti-Pope. Though Cyprian and Cornelius never met, they are forever celebrated liturgically together on September 16.

Cyprian's explicit ecclesiology focused primarily on the unity

of the local church. Given his own experience in Carthage and
Cornelius' in Rome, that is quite understandable. Both had to
oppose schismatic bishops, rejecting rigoristic dissidents on
the right and, in Cyprian's case at least, laxists as well at the
other end of the spectrum. Cyprian is certainly strong on the
unity of the bishops among themselves as well, but ultimately
it is difficult to see how his theory of the autonomy of each
local bishop can be reconciled with that wider unity. After
citing Mt. 16.18, he continues: "From this source flows the
appointment of bishops and the organization of the Church,
with bishop succeeding bishop down through the course of
time, so that the Church is founded upon the bishops and
every act of the Church is governed through these same appointed *leaders*" (*Ep.* 33.1).

The Chair of Peter

Cyprian makes considerable use of the image of Peter's
cathedra or chair.[9] Note however that it is important in his
theology of the local church. "God is one and Christ is one:
there is one Church and one chair founded, by the Lord's
authority, upon Peter. It is not possible that another altar can
be set up, or that a new priesthood can be appointed, over and
above this one altar and this one priesthood" (*Ep.* 43.5).

The *cathedra Petri* symbolism has been the source of much
misunderstanding and dispute. Perhaps it can be understood
more easily by looking at the special treatise he wrote to
defend both his own position as sole lawful bishop of Carthage
and that of Cornelius against Novatian, namely, the *De unitate
ecclesiae*,[10] or, as it was known in the Middle Ages, *On the
Simplicity of Prelates*. The chapter of most interest is the
fourth. Controversy has dogged this work because two versions
of this chapter exist. Since the Reformation, acceptance of one
version or the other has usually followed denominational lines.

Much of this has subsided in recent decades especially with
the work of Fr. Maurice Bevenot, an English Jesuit, who
devoted most of his scholarly life to this text. He championed
the suggestion of the English Benedictine, John Chapman,

that what we are dealing with here are two versions of a text, both of which were authored by Cyprian. This view has gained wide acceptance in recent decades. Not only did Cyprian write both but his theology of the Church is unchanged from the first to the second. He made textual changes because his earlier version was being misused.

The theology of the controverted chapter sees in Peter the symbol of unity, not from his being given greater authority by Christ for, as he says in both versions: ". . . a like power is given to all the Apostles" and, ". . . No doubt the others were all that Peter was." Yet Peter was given the power first: "Thus it is made clear that there is but one Church and one chair." The Chair of Peter then belongs to each lawful bishop in his own see. Cyprian holds the Chair of Peter in Carthage and Cornelius in Rome over against Novatian the would-be usurper. You must hold to this unity if you are to remain in the Church. "You cannot have God for your Father, if you no longer have the Church for your mother." (6) *Extra ecclesiam, salus non est* (*Ep.* 73.21). "He (Christ) put unanimity first; He gave precedence to peace and concord" (12).

Cyprian wants unity in the local church around the lawful bishop and unity among the bishops of the world who are "glued together" (*Ep.* 66.8). "Whereas, in truth, the Church forms one single whole; it is neither rent nor broken apart but is everywhere linked and banded together by the glue of the bishops sticking firmly to each other." (*Utique conexa et cohaerentium sibi invicem sacerdotum glutino copulata.*) He is concerned that he and other bishops in Africa be in communion and in communication with the lawful bishops in other parts of the Church (cf. e.g., *Ep.* 45 and *Ep.* 68.1, the case of Marcian of Arles). Yet it appears that this hoped for unity is inevitably undermined and contradicted by Cyprian's principle that "each bishop is responsible to God alone" (e.g., *Ep.* 30.1).[11]

The African tradition relied heavily on the calling of councils and Cyprian's practice greatly enhanced that role. He presided over several councils of Carthage. What was the obligation of each bishop in relation to the conciliar decrees? One sometimes gets the impression that if a bishop did not agree with Cyprian, the better part of wisdom for him would be not to attend the council. Cyprian's theory (or should we call it hope?) for unity among the bishops seems to bear within itself an intrinsic contradiction, one that comes to sad fruition in his clash with Stephen of Rome.

Apart from his good relations and harmony with Bishop Cornelius over the matter of the lapsed, what was Cyprian's basic view of the role, not of Peter as symbol of unity, but of Rome in the contemporary Church? Given what we have said above, it is clear that he did not see the bishop of Rome as his superior, except by way of honor, even though the lawful bishop of Rome also held the chair of Peter in an historical sense (*Ep.* 52.2). Another term frequently used by the Africans in speaking of the Church was "the root" (*radix*). Cyprian sometimes used the term in connection with Rome, leading some to assert that he regarded the Roman church as the "root". But in fact, in Cyprian's teaching, the Catholic Church as a whole is the root. So when he bade farewell to some Catholics travelling to Rome, he instructed them to be very careful about which group of Christians they contacted after their arrival in Rome. They must avoid schismatic groups like that of Novatian. They should contact and join the church presided over by Cornelius because it alone is the Catholic Church in Rome. In other words, Cyprian exhorted ". . . them to discern the womb and root (*matrix et radix*) of the Catholic Church and to cleave to it" (*Ep.* 48.3).[12]

On the other hand, there is at least one place where the symbolic role of Peter seems to meet and merge with the role of the contemporary bishop of Rome in the Church. This is in *Ep.* 59.14 from the year 252. Here Cyprian once again speaks of African visitors to Rome, only this time he is indignant because the travellers in question are some of the very troublemakers who have been causing so many difficulties for Cyprian in Carthage. He writes apologetically to Cornelius:

> . . . On the top of that they now have the audacity to sail off carrying letters from schismatics and outcasts from religion even to the chair of Peter, to the primordial church (*ecclesia principalis*) the very source of episcopal unity; and they do

> not stop to consider that they are carrying them to those same Romans whose faith was so praised and proclaimed by the Apostle, into whose company men without faith (*perfidia*) can, therefore, find no entry (*Ep.* 59.14).

He ends with a reference to Paul's comment in Romans but goes beyond the commonplace uttered by Paul. Is there really something out of the ordinary about the faith of the Roman Christians?

More significant is the apparent extension of the *cathedra Petri* symbolism. As we have seen, from the oneness of Peter and his chair episcopal unity (as it does or should exist) is derived. Extrapolating from the symbolism, the historic see of Peter, Rome, becomes the *Urkirche,* the primordial church. The historical Peter, who is also the symbol of unity, is buried there and exercises his influence still. Where does the symbolism end? Does it end? Is the Roman see the symbolic embodiment of unity for the whole Church the way a bishop himself is for each local community? It is difficult to know what theological conclusions, if any, to draw from such musings.

From what immediately follows in the same letter, however, it is clear that in Cyprian's mind, one theological conclusion he does not draw is that the bishop of Rome has authority which is superior to that of the African bishops. He asks what such dissidents hope to accomplish by their voyage.

> For it was a resolution enacted by us all and it is eminently right and just—that a man's case should be heard in the place where his offence was committed; and besides, each individual shepherd has been assigned a portion of the flock to rule and govern, knowing that one day he will be called upon to render an account to the Lord for this action. It is, therefore, totally improper that these men over whom we have charge should be tearing about, seeking to break up the harmony and concord that prevails among the bishops.... It is possible, I suppose, that this handful of desperate outlaws fancies that the authority of the bishops who have been appointed here in Africa is too slight to deal with their case (*Ep.* 59.14).

In other words, the Africans can take care of their own problems.

Cyprian and Stephen

The era of good feelings did not last. The election of Stephen as bishop of Rome in 254 changed things for the worse. Though no writings of his have survived, Stephen seems to have asserted his authority in both West and East. The fallout from the persecution was still being felt in the first two cases in which Cyprian came into conflict with Stephen. In the first instance, the two Spanish bishops,[13] of Leon and Astorga and Merida, had lapsed during the persecution of Decius and had been deposed. One of the them appealed to Stephen for reinstatement. At this point it should be remarked that it is not clear exactly what the bishop of Rome could do in Spain at this time. Could he command a reinstatement or merely urge and recommend it? In any event, once again Roman prestige in the West must be kept in mind. The faithful in Spain were upset and wrote to Cyprian for advice. Backed by an African council, Cyprian told them not to take their former bishops back. They had been correctly deposed and new bishops duly elected. The latter were to be maintained in office. Cyprian excused Stephen on the grounds that he had been misinformed by the deposed bishop. Despite this Roman prestige, in certain cases Cyprian did not hesitate to oppose its decisions and urge others to do the same.

Another case came at about the same time from the fractious world of southern Gaul. Marcian, bishop of Arles, had taken a hard line against the lapsed, even refusing them reconciliation on their death beds. In his letter 68 to Stephen, Cyprian complained that nothing had been done about Marcian's case. He intimated that Marcian had allied himself with Novatian. In this case, Cyprian upbraided Stephen for *not* taking action. As with Spain, the status of Roman authority in southern Gaul is not clear. Apparently, Stephen cannot simply depose Marcian directly; he is to tell the Gallic bishops to do something. Despite Cyprian's statement a few lines earlier, one would have to conjecture that in fact while Bishop Faustinus of Lyons had complained to Cyprian about Marcian, not all the Gallic bishops agreed with him. Once again, we do not know the outcome of this, but Cyrian is not slow to tell Stephen where his duty lies.

These letters are noteworthy as well in their description of the process for electing a bishop (*Ep.* 67.5)[14] and the consciousness of solidarity among the Church's bishops and the duty that each has to see to it that problems in any region are taken care of (*Ep.* 68.3). "... The large body of bishops joined by the bond of mutual concord and the chain of unity so that, if anyone of our college should attempt to engage in heresy and wound and lay waste the flock of Christ, the others, as useful and merciful shepherds, should assist and should assemble the sheep of the Lord into the flock." Cyprian asks that when the new bishop of Arles is in place, his name should be conveyed to all other bishops, "... that we may know to whom to direct our brethren and to whom we should write" (*Ep.* 68.5). It is of utmost importance to be in communion with the right bishops (cf. also *Ep.* 66.8).

These minor interventions had scarcely passed when the major theological controversy of Cyprian's final years came to the fore. This concerned the rebaptism of heretics.[15] Here Cyprian's narrow ecclesiology is most evident. Outside the Church, no salvation? One might as well have said, no grace. The controversy arose because certain people, having been baptized for the first time by followers of Novatian, now wished to join the Catholic Church. What to do? When someone noted that the followers of Novatian were not heretical; they had the same creed, the same liturgy, the same baptism as Catholics, Cyprian replied without hesitation: it avails them nothing because they do not have the Church (*Ep.* 69.7; 71). Their priests can give nothing so that when such people become Catholics, they must be (re)baptized validly for the first time because for the first time they are entering the Catholic Church. This view was commonly held in Asia minor and Syria but had been maintained in North Africa only since the time of bishop Agrippinus of Carthage c. 220 A.D.

Stephen, on the other hand, with the agreement of the

churches of Alexandria and Palestine, held that heretical baptisms were valid but inefficacious. When our Novatianist became a Catholic in Rome, he was not rebaptized but his earlier baptism was considered efficacious only when hands had been imposed on him, as on a penitent, and he was restored to full Catholic communion. The progress or degeneration of this exchange between Cyprian and Stephen went on from 254-56 and became increasingly bitter in tone.

From Cyprian's point of view, Stephen's position not only made no sense, it undermined the Church. To concede the validity of the baptism of a dissident group, was essentially to concede that they were the Church. Cyprian was even more incensed when Stephen wrote to him: *Nihil innovetur nisi quod traditum est (Ep.* 74.1).[16] No innovations! In a time when everyone claimed to be a traditionalist, this was a serious insult. Cyprian hit back with an almost equally well-known phrase: *Nam consuetudo sine veritate, vetustas erroris est* (*Ep.* 74.9). A false custom simply means that you have been doing the wrong thing for a long time. Jesus said: "I am the Truth", not, "I am the custom." As in the Quartodeciman controversy, we find a clash of customs long held in different parts of the Church. The Roman view is not tolerant of differing customs; as later Roman letters will claim, it alone has preserved the apostolic tradition unchanged.

There was an asymmetry in the reciprocal demands. With his views on episcopal autonomy, Cyprian was in no position to tell the Roman church that it must adopt the African practices. Stephen, on the other hand, very clearly told the Africans to stop doing what they were doing. A letter from an outsider, a Greek bishop, Firmilian of Caesarea in Cappadocia, climaxed the angry exchange (*Ep.* 75). As mentioned above, Asia Minor agreed with the African position and Firmilian's letter gives an indication that Stephen had turned his attention to them as well (*Ep.* 75.25), just as Victor had done in the Quartodeciman controversy nearly sixty years earlier. Firmilian, who had spent some time in exile and had taken in Origen's lectures at Caesarea in Palestine, was bitter and sarcastic in his tone of rejection of Stephen's views. He remarked, for instance, that Stephen's unkindness had at least the good result of bringing Cyprian and himself together (2). Stephen is "bold and insolent" (3), "manifestly stupid" (17), "a disgrace to Peter and Paul" (6), with a "slippery, fickle and uncertain mind" (25). Like Cyprian, he accused Stephen of conceding the reality of other churches by accepting their baptism. He finds it ironic that:

> He who so glories in the place of his episcopate and contends that he has the succession from Peter on whom the foundation of the Church was established, should introduce many other rocks and constitute new buildings of many churches while he maintains by his authority that baptism is there (*Ep.* 75.17).[17]

Since we do not have Stephen's own letters, such a comment, however sarcastic, is precious insofar as it indicates Stephen's own view of the source of his authority, the authority by which he directs not only Carthage but far distant Cappadocia to change their basic customs and conform to Roman ways. This is the first known appeal of a Roman bishop to Peter's authority, indeed to the classical Petrine Gospel texts. But we must note as well that Firmilian not only does not accept the claim, he seems never to have heard of it before. He notes for example that in many liturgical customs, Rome differs from Jerusalem (6). There are variations from one church to another, "And yet, on account of this, there has been no withdrawal at all from the peace and unity of the Catholic Church"(6). "How can you live in communion with such a person?"(25). Rome insists on uniformity but other bishops, such as Irenaeus and Firmilian, note that all have gotten along well up until now with varying customs.

It has often been asked whether a break was made between Rome and Carthage over this issue before Stephen's death in 257. Most people have been reluctant to grant it. Augustine always argued against the Donatists that Cyprian was a lover of unity who refused to break that unity. Yet some of the language of Firmilian's letter is very harsh. He reports that Stephen had called Cyprian "a false Christ, a false Apostle and a treacherous laborer" (25). To which Firmilian replied: You

(Stephen) are the one who is these things. He reports further that when Cyprian sent representatives to Rome in the hope of calming the dispute, not only would Stephen not see them, he directed the Roman Christians not to allow them into their homes, a serious breach in the tradition of Christian hospitality (26). One final sarcastic comment of Firmilian on this: "Such humility of mind and meekness!" (*Ep.* 75.25).

Such a sad state of affairs certainly seems like a schism. But Stephen died; in the persecution of Valerian, Cyprian was exiled (257) and then executed (258).[18] The practices of rebaptism in both North Africa and Asia Minor continued unchanged into the fourth century, so that once more Roman demands for uniformity do not seem to have accomplished their purpose. This early assertion of Roman authority does not appear to have moved Firmilian, and its stated basis was unknown to him. Even Cyprian the westerner who honored the Roman see did not admit Rome's authority to demand a change in the African practice. The council he presided over in Carthage in September 256 agreed with him on this issue.

His own opening remarks sum up his views on this question of a world leadership for the Church:

> For neither does any of us set himself up as a bishop of bishops nor by tyrannical terror force his colleagues to a necessity of obeying; inasmuch as every bishop, in the free use of his liberty and power, has the right of forming his own judgment, and can no more be judged by another than he himself can judge another.
>
> But we must all await the judgment of Our Lord Jesus Christ, who alone has the power both of setting us in the government of his Church, and of judging of our acts therein (*Sententiae episcoporum*).

The Rise of Donatism[19]

As mentioned in the previous chapter, the period from Cyprian to the great persecution, more than forty years, is a blank spot for the most part. We next see African and Roman interests come together at the end of that persecution, when Constantine became emperor of the West in 312. If Constantine had begun to favor Christianity in the hope of using it to foster unity in the empire, he must have been quickly disabused of such an idea. Not long after coming to power in Rome, he found that the North African church was anything but united. The group known as the Donatists petitioned the emperor to appoint judges to review the justice of their case against Caecilian, bishop of Carthage, whom they rejected for having been ordained by a *traditor*. They suggested that Gallic bishops be brought into the case as impartial judges since *traditio*[20] had not been an issue in Gaul during the persecution.

Constantine, perhaps at the urging of bishop Ossius, selected three Gallic bishops but asked bishop Miltiades of Rome to preside over the hearing. The three Gallic bishops went to Rome but the ensuing hearing became in effect a small Roman council of fifteen Italian bishops presided over by Miltiades. Both sides were heard, and the Donatist case was rejected. They refused to accept the decision as they would continue to reject similar negative decisions by other bodies in the future. Perhaps they had grounds for an appeal in that they had not been given the kind of judges they had asked for.

The Roman conciliar decision, after their appeal, was set aside and a large council was called for at Arles in southern Gaul in 314.[21] As some commentators have noted, Constantine does not seem to have had further dealings with Miltiades. When he moved East in 324 and found the Church there also in danger of disunity, his immediate reaction was to call for a large council, Nicaea in 325. The bishop of Rome did not attend the council of Arles whose outcome was the same as that of the Roman council. The bishops at Arles wrote respectfully to bishop Sylvester, noting that he had been "by no means able to leave that region where the Apostles daily sit and their blood without ceasing bears witness to the glory of God." Rome's position as the center of communion for the Western Church is shown in the council's expectation that "they (the conciliar decisions) should be brought to the knowledge of all especially by you."

Constantine's efforts first at reconciliation, then at coercion did not succeed in reuniting the Church in North Africa. For the group that preached that the true Church is the one which is persecuted but does not itself persecute, coercion would be welcomed as an apologetic plus. The Donatists were in fact a mass church in North Africa that refused to adapt to the new reality of the Constantinian era. They maintained the rhetoric of the sect at enmity with the world. Despite this anomalous existence, they seemed to have easily outshone the Catholics throughout most of the fourth century. Their superior leadership in the persons of Donatus and Parmenian may have been the decisive factor. Catholic leadership appears weak before the arrival in the last decade of the century of that winning combination of Aurelius of Carthage and Augustine of Hippo.

Optatus of Milevis

The one Catholic protagonist whose work survives is Optatus,[22] bishop of Milevis in Numidia. His treatise against Parmenian was written c. 367 with a revised and enlarged edition c. 385. Augustine later made use of Optatus' historical documentation purporting to show the innocence of Catholics accused of *traditio* at the end of the great persecution and, on the contrary, the guilt and hypocrisy of the Donatist founders. The theological arguments were also significant both concerning the sacraments and also catholicity. As noted earlier, Cyprian's theology of the Church was largely concerned with the local church. This was no longer adequate because it was now a question of a regional schism. The North African system was not one of geographically extensive dioceses. Here every little village had a bishop. And in this time of schism, the fourth century, almost every little village had its Catholic and Donatist bishops. In rare cases, one group so dominated that the other did not dare field a bishop.

In this new situation, Optatus' theology needed to put forward a revised argument for unity and, of course, it had to extend, not only beyond the local church, but beyond the region as well. His argument from the marks of the Church, a notation suggested by his opponent Parmenian, is not helpful here. Optatus' appeal (and Augustine's after him) must be to a geographic catholicity of the Church beyond Africa. The Donatist assertion that they were the last remnant of the true Church surviving only in North Africa, the rest of the Church having perished by entering into communion with the North African *traditores,* was ridiculed as absurd in itself and as a repudiation of the messianic prophecies that Christ would come to have the whole world as his heritage. The Donatist position was ludicrous, about as valid or credible on the world scale as that of the Donatist splinter group, the Rogatists, on the African level. Augustine would later mock the Rogatists when he wrote that they "sit in Cartenna (a small city on the North African coast far to the west of Hippo) with ten Rogatists who are left and you say (to such Messianic prophecies) 'Let it not be. Let it not be'" (*Ep.* 93.20).

The test of such geographic catholicity was: is your church in communion with the rest of the Church? For Westerners that meant: Are you in communion with the Roman church? Surprisingly the Donatists could answer in the affirmative. Optatus, however, soon showed such a reply to be at best, naive, at worst, a subterfuge. Many Africans had migrated to Rome. Inevitably, during the fourth century, some of them were Donatists. Probably as a pastoral measure, the African Donatists sent one of their number, Victor of Garba, to minister to these Roman Donatists. He was a bishop and had successors, all of them, to be sure, African immigrants. But, technically, there was a Donatist succession in Rome. Optatus asked if any of them were ever allowed in the Roman basilicas. With that foolish objection disposed of, the answer to Optatus' original question was obviously negative. The Donatists were not in communion with Rome.

But Rome was not the sole criterion of communion. He asked if they were in communion with the Eastern churches to which Paul had written, Paul whose epistles the Donatists still read publicly. What about the churches in Asia Minor to which John wrote at the beginning of the Apocalypse? The answer in both cases was once again in the negative. The argument from geographic catholicity would be used again and again by Augustine against the Donatists.

The work of Optatus, little known as it is, was a turning point. Cyprian's use of "Chair of Peter", as we have seen, was largely symbolic. Optatus still began his argument with the same mindset. In Book I.10, in arguing over who was responsible for the initial schism, Optatus stated: "Nor was it Caecilian who separated himself from the chair of Peter or (*vel*) from the chair of Cyprian. . . . " Catholic commentators have usually interpreted this as referring to two distinct separations, from Rome (Chair of Peter) and from Carthage (Chair of Cyprian). They called attention to the fact that the "Chair of Peter" was named first. In fact, I believe, here Optatus is using Cyprianic terminology. The Chair of Peter and Chair of Cyprian are one and the same, to be occupied only by the lawful bishop of Carthage who is, of course, Caecilian, not Majorinus.

But in Book II, where most of the argumentation about geographic catholicity takes place, I believe that Optatus truly turns the corner. In discussing the primary "mark of the Church" (*dos ecclesiae*), the *cathedra* and the *angelus,* the lawful bishop who occupies the *cathedra,* he begins his argument:

> You cannot then deny that you do know that upon Peter first in the city of Rome was bestowed the episcopal cathedra on which sat Peter the head of all the Apostles (for which reason he was called Cephas), that, in this one Cathedra, unity should be preserved by all, lest the other Apostles might claim each for himself separate cathedras, so that he who should set up a second Cathedra against the unique Cathedra would already be a schismatic and a sinner (Bk. II.2).

This passage too can and should be understood in the symbolic sense of Cyprian. But then Optatus launches out into the list of the bishops of Rome up to his own time, ending with Siricius (384-99), "who today is our colleague with whom the whole world through the intercourse of letters of peace, agrees with us in one bond of communion." (Bk. II.3)

He closes this section by challenging the Donatists to show the origin of their cathedra and immediately follows with the attack on their Donatist line of bishops in Rome. I believe that this section should be studied in connection with Cyprian's *Ep.* 59.14, where the symbolic joins and melds with the contemporary reality. Rome, "the source whence the unity of the bishops took its rise"—contemporary Rome or the symbolic chair of Peter? In the light of the importance of being in communion with Rome for Optatus' argument against the Donatists, the contemporary significance begins to take on greater importance than the older symbolic meaning.

Augustine of Hippo[23]

If one were to read only the youthful works of Augustine, from the time of his conversion, the *Dialogues* of Cassiciacum for instance, one might never hear that Donatism existed or was a great problem for the Catholic Church in Africa. but when he entered the pastoral ministry in Hippo as a priest in 391 and a bishop from 395, he quickly had to face the challenge. A man of many talents, he, like Arius before him, even wrote a psalm for people to sing in church. This way they could learn about the history and theology of the Catholic rejection of Donatism. The refrain echoed: "All you who care about peace, now judge the truth for yourselves."

As Augustine found his arguments concerning geographic catholicity in Optatus, so his use of the figure of Peter frequently seems to follow the line of Optatus and even Cyprian. Against the Manichaeans who urged potential converts to accept the writings of Mani as Scripture he asked: "Why should I?" He will stay where he is. Why? "The consent of peoples and nations keeps me in the Church. So does her authority. . . . The succession of priests (i.e., bishops) keeps me, beginning from the very seat of the Apostle Peter down to the present episcopate" (*Contra ep. Fund.* IV.5).[24] The Chair of Peter is the place whence, as Cyprian put it, "the unity of the bishops took its rise." Like Optatus, he gives the list of Roman bishops when challenged by a Donatist concerning the bishops of Cirta

(Numidia) (*Ep.* 53.2, c. 400 A.D.). As he says in his psalm mentioned above: "Count the bishops since Peter himself sat; See how in that list the fathers have succeeded one another; This is the rock which the proud gates of Hell cannot conquer" (*Psalmus contra partem Donati,* vv. 236-39).

In debating with Petilian, the Donatist bishop of Cirta, he remarked that Anastasius sits in the chair of Peter today in Rome but he adds that John sits in the chair of James in Jerusalem as well and that the Donatists are not in communion with either (*Contra litteras Petiliani,* LI.118). Augustine's interpretation of the role of Peter is not a simple one. To illustrate this, recall at the end of his life, in his *Retractationes* (I.20.1), commenting on a now lost anti-Donatist work, he noted that he had interpreted the rock of Mt. 16.18 as referring to Peter himself at times but at other times as referring to Christ. He ended by leaving the interpretation of the rock to the free choice of the reader. *Harum duarum autem sententiarum quae sit probabilior, eligat lector.* For Augustine, Peter himself, and not just the Chair of Peter, was a symbol of the Church. When Peter speaks or is spoken to, the Church is speaking or is being addressed. Peter speaks *unus pro omnibus.* As Augustine wrote in *Sermo Guelf.* XVI.2,[25] "When the Lord questioned Peter, he was questioning us; he was questioning the Church. That you may know that Peter bears the figure of the Church, recall the section of the Gospels: Thou art Peter. . . . " Peter is the *figura* of the Church, the principal one but not the only one. Depending on what Scripture passage Augustine is preaching on, others may also serve as the symbol of the Church, for example, Mary Magdalene (*Sermo* 245.4) or in *Sermo* 77, both the Canaanite woman and the woman with the hemorrhage.

If his reference to Roman authority in the context of the Donatist controversy is small and does not appear to go beyond Optatus, the development of the Pelagian controversy in a later decade did eventuate in a direct appeal to Roman authority. This was the sole significant heresy which arose in the West, an anthropological controversy involving the God-man relationship. Augustine was the heart and soul of the controversy.

Pelagius[26] was a British monk who gained notoriety in Rome as a preacher of penance, urging Roman Christians to live up to their baptismal commitment and to raise themselves from their moral mediocrity by renewed resolution and effort. Pelagius and his associate Celestius, like many others, had fled to North Africa after the sack of Rome by Alaric in 410. Celestius' views were condemned when he sought ordination. He was ordained not long after in Ephesus. Pelagius' and Celestius' views were approved by two small councils in Palestine (Diospolis and Jerusalem) in 415.

When the Africans got wind of this reversal, they determined not only to reiterate their own condemnation as they soon did at councils in Carthage and Milevis but sent those results to Rome asking for the confirmation of Pope Innocent. To strengthen their case, a third, private letter was sent by Aurelius, Augustine and their friends. The Africans were quite confident of their own views but they realized that their own regional condemnation could once again be neutralized by approval forthcoming from another regional council. But approval of their position by the ecumenical authority of Rome would eliminate that danger.

To further their purpose, they wrote letters couched in a style calculated to be favorably received in Rome. Thus not surprisingly there was a good bit of *captatio benevolentiae* in the style of these letters. This aims to flatter the addressee in order to improve one's chances of getting what one wants. So, for example, the council of Carthage asked that "the authority of the apostolic see be added to the statutes of our mediocrity" (*Ep.* 175.2).[27] The private letter asked Pope Innocent to test to see "whether our littleness flows from the same head of waters as your abundance..." (*Ep.* 177.19).

They were overjoyed when Innocent's replies to the three letters were favorable to their requests, and a Roman condemnation of Pelagius' teaching was added to the weight of the earlier African disapproval. Innocent's replies contain the usual Roman reminders of Roman authority. Innocent applauds the Carthaginian decision to follow "the example of ancient tradition" and the "institutions of the Fathers" by seeing to it "that whatever is done, even though it be in distant provinces, should not be ended until it comes to the knowledge of this see. . . " (*Ep.* 181.1). Rome praised the Numidians for knowing that "the answers to questions always flow through all provinces from the apostolic spring" (*Ep.* 182.2). "Equally as often as questions of faith are to be ventilated, I think all our brothers and fellow bishops ought to refer to none but Peter, i.e., to the author of their name and office. . . " (*Ep.* 182.2).

We just mentioned that the first letter to Innocent, that of the council of Carthage of 416, asked Innocent to verify that their little trickle came from the same source (Christ?, the Gospel?) as his own mighty stream. The implication seemed to be that while both Rome and Carthage came from the same source, Rome's torrent was so much greater than Carthage's. But, in his reply, Innocent seems to shift the metaphor just enough so that there is no longer simply a comparison of amplitude of flow, but the Roman see itself has become the source, the fountainhead. "Thus, just as all waters come forth from their natural source and flow through all parts of the world, keeping the purity of their source, so all other churches may draw from *this* source knowledge of what they are to teach, whom they are to absolve. . . " (*Ep.* 181.1).[28]

It was at this point that the famous words of Augustine were uttered (as misquoted): *Roma locuta est; causa finita est.* Actually he said (*sermo.* 131): "Already two councils on this question have been sent to the apostolic see; and replies have also come from there. The case is closed; would that the error might sometime be finished as well." But, beyond any quibbling over precise words, the greater irony is the use of this "quotation" in later centuries. We have all heard it used in the following sense: Rome has made its decision. All further discussion must cease.

Pope Innocent died about six weeks after his reply to the Africans. His successor, the short-lived but controversial Zosimus, reversed or was perceived as reversing, Innocent's condemnation. The Africans were first astounded, then furious. They shot back, like so many in the future, that they would stand firm with Innocent's condemnation.

Zosimus apparently astonished in turn by the vehemence of

the African reaction, wrote back in a masterpiece of ambiguity. The letter (*Quamvis Patrum* of 21 March 418) complains that the Africans must have misunderstood if they thought that he was approving Celestius. Not so. He was simply suggesting a slower and more deliberate re-study of the issues. This backing and filling was accompanied by a new and more decisive statement of Roman authority. "Such being our authority . . . that no one can revise our decision. . . ." While there is some debate over who acted first, the Pope or the emperor, the African determination prevailed and the Pelagians were condemned both by Church and State. Zosimus sent around his *epistola tractoria.*

A small number of Italian bishops led by the young bishop of Eclanum, Julian,[29] refused to agree and were deposed. Thus began the final decade of Augustine's life, marred by an increasingly infuriating personal debate between Julian and himself. As in the case of Cyprian versus Stephen over the issue of the Spanish bishops, Augustine seemed to go out of his way to shield Zosimus from any blame. He portrayed Zosimus as a very merciful prelate who did not wish to strike Celestius with a severe sentence (*De pecc. orig.* 7).[30] They were treated with greater leniency than the stricter discipline of the Church required (*Contra duas epp. Pel.* II.5). And writing to Julian himself: Zosimus did not retreat from the decision of his predecessor Innocent (*Contra Jul.* VI.37).

On his many visits to Italy on behalf of the African episcopate, bishop Alypius of Thagaste would gather up the latest writings of Julian and bring them back to Africa for Augustine to answer. During the time of Zosimus' successor, Boniface, Augustine wrote: "Surely, then provided the stability of the most ancient and robust faith was maintained, whatever in the meanwhile was done more leniently with Celestius was the most merciful persuasion of correction, not the most pernicious approval of wickedness" (*Contra duas epp. Pel.* II.5). This concerted effort on the part of Augustine to put the best face on Zosimus's vacillations shows Augustine's respect for the apostolic see. We must, however, keep in mind as well his need to uphold the authority of Innocent's condemnation. To undermine the authority of one pope (Zosimus) would not help to safeguard that of his predecessor Innocent.

Apiarius

There is yet another case which needs to be discussed. It is much more a case of canon law than of theology, and it concerns the African episcopate as a whole rather than Augustine alone. It involves primarily the right of African bishops to appeal to Rome. This issue was brought to the fore by the appeal of a priest named Apiarius[31] who was disciplined by his bishop, Urban of Sicca Veneria, formerly prior of Augustine's monastery in Hippo. There seems to be no clear and definitive answer to the question of the *status quo ante* on episcopal appeals. A sensible guess might be that, even if frowned upon in Africa, in fact, they happened albeit fairly rarely. Episcopal canons told bishops to appeal within Africa, probably because sometimes some bishops in fact went to Rome. One weak spot in the African position was that its canons provided for no appeal process for priests and lower clergy. This opening for Roman objection was closed at the last minute by an African council in May 418. When Rome sent Apiarius back to Africa, three delegates led by bishop Faustinus of Potentia, accompanied him. They brought a document with four Roman demands. The main demand was that African bishops be allowed to appeal to Rome. Apiarius himself would be allowed to continue to minister provided that he moved to a distant town. By the time this council of May 419 met, Zosimus was dead and Boniface elected his successor in Rome.

The Apiarius affair was the object of much study and attention from French scholars in the seventeenth and eighteenth centuries because, insofar as the ancient canons stressed African autonomy against Roman interference, they were perceived as supporting Gallican autonomy against Roman centralization. The ancient Church sought to safeguard both the prerogatives of the local church and the needs of the wider Church. In its fifth canon, the council of Nicaea had tried to protect the autonomy of the discipline of the local church from being undermined because other local churches ignored or even scorned it. The local church and its discipline were to be respected. Cases were to be settled as far as possible where the alleged crime had been committed. On the other hand, a

local bishop might be an unreasonable tyrant and thus canon
five tried to protect the rights of the individual by having local
or regional councils meet twice a year to review these cases.
The Africans appealed to this ideal, "And now we pray your
holiness to cause us to observe the acts drawn up by the
fathers at Nicaea and to enforce among yourselves there those
things which they brought in the commonitory"(Letter of the
Council of Carthage of May 31, 419, to Pope Boniface, 2).[32]

The second issue originated in a serious case of historical
amnesia. Rome claimed that the canons of Nicaea authorized
bishops to appeal to Rome. The Africans denied any knowledge of such a canon in Nicaea. In fact what was at issue were
the appeal canons of Sardica (c. 343). The Africans had forgotten them completely; the Romans had forgotten Sardica
but kept the canons and added them to the Nicene canons.
Although suspicious, the Africans agreed to observe the appeal
provision until such time as authentic copies of the Greek
canons of Nicaea should be sent to Carthage from the East. In
the interim they asked to be treated by Rome with respect and
not with insolence.

It has been argued that the various vague references to
appeals of African bishops to Rome all happened within this
brief period before the Greek texts of Nicaea were received in
Africa. This seems most unlikely. One case of an episcopal
appeal concerns Augustine directly. This emerged from the
period between the two halves of the Apiarius affair, c. 423.
When the Donatists were forced back into Catholic unity after
411, there arose a need for more clergy. For an area which he
had administered himself up until recently, Fussala near
Hippo, Augustine selected a very young monk, Antoninus,[33]
to be the first bishop. This turned out to be one of the most
disastrous decisions of his life. The young man, who had never
exercised any pastoral responsibility, seemed to have had as
his great passion to build himself a nice house. This was to be
accomplished by threatening, robbing and fleecing his new
flock. The outcry brought Antoninus' deposition, but he too
appealed to Rome, to Pope Boniface. We do not know the
final outcome. Augustine pleads for the distressed people of
Fussala, admitting his own guilt and chagrin in the affair (*Ep.*

209 to Pope Celestine). In one of the new letters (20*), Augustine details at great length Antoninus' depredations and the episcopal comings and goings in Numidia brought about by the case and the Roman appeal.

The climax of the Apiarius case came in an incredible replay of the first half in a council held in 424 under Pope Celestine. Apiarius, ministering in his new assignment, the seaport of Tabraca, was deposed by his new bishop. He appealed to Rome and the very same delegates reappeared on the Africans' doorstep. The great difference this time was that during the council Apiarius broke down and confessed that all the charges were true. This led the African bishops to write a letter that must go down as one of the most angry ever written to Rome (*Optaremus*).[34] "Therefore with all due respect we earnestly beseech that in future you do not readily admit to hearing persons coming hence, or further choose to receive to communion those who have been excommunicated by us, because you, venerable sir, will readily perceive that this has been defined even by the Nicene council" (2). They argue that the prohibition of appeals should apply *especially* to bishops! The care of the clergy has been entrusted to the bishops. "And they did not think that the grace of the Holy Spirit would be lacking in any province for the priests of Christ to discern wisely the right and to hold it firmly...; unless by chance there is anyone who believes that God can inspire a single individual with justice and refuse it to numberless priests assembled in council." They added that the Pope should resist sending delegates to other parts of the Church since that would "introduce the smoky pride of the world into the Church of Christ..." (5). And above all, may they never have to endure the likes of Faustinus again! These words, as I noted, were among the strongest that we know of from bishops of one region to Rome. Thus canonical legislation from African councils forbidding appeals "across the sea" should come as no surprise. Indeed some have claimed that the words "across the sea" were added later as a euphemism to replace the blunter prohibition "that no one may appeal to the Roman church."[35]

The Apiarius affair is a prime bit of evidence for those who would claim that the African tradition resisted Roman intervention at every step. They point out, for example, that the Africans ultimately, because of their own need, came to accept some Donatist clergy under certain conditions into the Catholic Church in the capacity of clergy despite objections from "across the sea." Some have argued therefore that Roman intervention was kept to a minimum.[36]

The new letters of Augustine[37] in particular seem to cast doubt on this view. Remember that Augustine himself at the age of 64 had embarked on the longest land journey of his life to Caesarea in Mauretania, far to the West on the North African coast in 418 on unspecified business for the Pope. Shortly after this visit, at the end of 419 or the beginning of 420, the issue of the succession to bishop Deuterius of Caesarea came up. There were problems and in letters 23*A and 22*, Augustine comments that "ill feelings and unavoidable necessity" will require that Rome and Carthage be consulted on this issue. This might be considered a question of some significance but another new letter (9*) tells of what appears to be a very minor issue. A man of some importance was flogged at the order of some priests because he had kidnapped and raped a nun. Augustine, writing to Alypius, simply notes that Pope Celestine wanted those who were the cause of the beating to be punished.

It would seem then that in fact Roman interventions were more common than had earlier been believed. The African bishops normally wished to maintain their autonomy and their own authority but sought Roman help when it suited their purpose or their need. Did Roman authority on the other hand, generally restrain itself or did it seek to take advantage of appeals from discontented priests and lower clergy in order to find occasions to insert itself into the affairs of the African church? We can record actions but the assessing of motivation is nearly impossible.

It has been noted that Augustine himself was not among the signers of the 424 letter (*Optaremus*) to Pope Celestine. Why not? Because he thought it too strong? or simply because he was not present? It has been suggested that in fact Augustine was more favorable to Roman authority than the majority of the African episcopate. He is always respectful, as we have seen above, in a variety of cases, but ultimately he seems to have held to councils as the organs for the settling of disputed questions within the Church.[38] He writes for example that "...the best opinion was established, to the removal of all doubts, by a general council of the whole world" (*De bapt.* I.9). He speaks about councils with greatest frequency during the Donatist controversy. For one thing, he claimed that the Donatists did not have the excuse concerning re-baptism that Cyprian had because the latter died before a general council had settled the question. He was never able to identify this council, however.

The best-known passage on this issue comes from the treatise on baptism (II.3.4). Here the context is the relativizing of Cyprian's prestige, his views, his councils to which the Donatists were constantly appealing. Scripture, he observed: "... stands above all later letters of the bishops ... that the letters of bishops which have been written or shall be written since the closing of the canon are liable to be refuted, either by discourse of someone wiser, or by the weightier authority and more learned prudence of other bishops, or by councils; and that those councils which are held in the several districts or provinces must yield without doubt to the authority of plenary councils which are formed for the whole Christian world; and that even of the plenary councils the earlier are often corrected by the later, when by some experience things are brought to light which were concealed and that becomes known which lay hid...."

Elsewhere I have argued in detail Augustine's views of authority in the Church and that, in my opinion, the council was the primary instrument for settling controversies. What kind of council? Nicaea was the only ecumenical council he knew from history. The West had not yet come to accept the council of Constantinople of 381 as ecumenical. All-African councils were frequent and were also called general councils. Could one council correct an earlier one, in the sense that the earlier council had been in error on a matter of faith? Or was it a case of "improving" (*emendari*)? I believe that Augustine had great respect for the Roman church whose antiquity and apostolic origins made it outshine by far other churches in the West. But as with Cyprian, the African collegial and conciliar tradition was to be preferred most of the time.

IV

Ambrose and Jerome

Of the four great Western Fathers, three lived at the end of the fourth century. Of these, we have discussed the greatest, Augustine in his African context. Gregory the Great at the end of the sixth century we leave appropriately to the very end. At this point then, we shall discuss the two that remain, Ambrose and Jerome.

Ambrose of Milan

Ambrose,[1] though born of an aristocratic and well-placed Christian family, had, like many of his generation, grown to adulthood without being baptized, though he was raised as a Christian. He was governor of the northern Italian province of Liguria-Aemilia with good prospects for higher rank in the service of the state. But in late 373, Auxentius the Arian bishop of the northern metropolis of Mediolanum (Milan) died. As the official responsible for maintaining law and order, Ambrose was concerned about the possibility of disturbances arising between the contending parties during the election of a successor. The legend of Ambrose's election is well-known. He had to be baptized first of all before he could begin the reception of orders. As with so many others in a similar situation, he felt keenly the lack of any theological preparation. But as the son of a high-ranking family, he had had a solid classical education. The Neoplatonic philosopher-priest Simplicianus,

* Notes for this chapter can be found on p. 159

who also figures in Augustine's life-story, took Ambrose in hand. But, in the judgment of some, Ambrose ever after seemed overly dependent in his preaching and writing on the tradition of allegorizing exegesis found in Origen and his Eastern heirs.

Milan was an increasingly large and important center. At this time it was the residence of the western emperor. It became the metropolitan see of northern Italy. With the forceful personality of Ambrose, its influence was felt not only all over northern Italy but also to the west in southern Gaul and to the east in what is now northern and central Yugoslavia. Ambrose made it his particular mission to root out the last vestiges of western Arianism found in Illyricum. He was then something of a phenomenon, threatening to throw into the shade and rival the Roman see, even though the bishops of Rome at that period, Damasus and Siricius, were themselves strong characters. Ambrose's biographer, Paulinus, said of him what the Roman bishops were saying of themselves, namely. "There was in him the concern for all the churches."[2] In summary, while Ambrose felt great respect and admiration for the Roman see, he also seems at times to have gone out of his way to establish a separate and clearly identifiable stance for himself and his see. In retrospect, his positions were at times clearly less desirable than the Roman stance on some issues.

Ambrose frequently convoked councils of local bishops. He ordained such minor lights as Gaudentius of Brescia and Chromatius of Aquileia. In the year after his death, his successor for a brief period, the elderly Simplicianus, ordained Maximus the first bishop for Turin. Ambrose made Milan one of the major sees of the West, one frequently consulted along with Rome as one of the *ecclesiae transmarinae* questioned by the Africans or by Eastern prelates seeking western support. In 376, he travelled to Sirmium in Pannonia secunda to make sure that another Arian would not be chosen as bishop. He was successful, and his candidate, the orthodox Anemius, was elected. He seems to have hoped to exercise influence on a large scale as well.

The council of Aquileia of 381,[3] which seems to have been touted as the western equivalent of the council of Constantinople of that year, took positions on some Eastern questions. It reiterated Western support for Paulinus of Antioch in the Meletian schism in that city, even as Meletius himself with wide support in the East was presiding over the very same council of Constantinople. An even more dubious cause supported at Aquileia was that of Maximus the Cynic who, with Alexandrian support, had unsuccessfully attempted to subvert Gregory of Nazianzus in Constantinople.

Supporters of the Spanish heretic Priscillian[4] had appealed both to Damasus in Rome as well as to Ambrose in Milan. Finding no support here, they made the fatal mistake of appealing to the usurping western emperor Magnus Maximus in Trier. By sentencing these Christian dissidents to be executed, he assured himself a place in history as the first civil official to condemn people to death for heresy.

Ambrose of Milan was a person of note in the Church. There could be no question of any divergence on matters of faith between Milan and Rome but there were differences of policy on how to approach current problems. Rome was the center of communion, as Ambrose was well aware. When describing the behavior of his brother Satyrus who had been shipwrecked in Sardinia, he reported that his brother, concerned about the presence of Luciferian fanatics, had inquired of the local bishop whether he (the bishop) was in communion with the Catholic bishops., i.e., with the Roman church (*De excessu fratris*[5] 21.47 of February 378).

At the council of Aquileia in 381 a request was forwarded to the emperor Gratian asking that he take steps to quell continuing opposition in Rome to Pope Damasus on the part of the followers of Ursinus, his rival for the episcopate fifteen years earlier.

> It is fitting that your Clemency be requested not to allow the Roman church, the head of the whole Roman world and that sacred faith of the Apostles, to be disturbed, for thence flow to all the rights of venerable communion. (*Inde enim in omnes venerandae communionis iura dimanant*).... We therefore entreat you to get rid of this most importunate person and thus restore the sense of security

which has been interrupted, both to our bishops and to the people of Rome who, ever since the Prefect of the City has sent in his report, have remained in uncertainty and suspense.

It should be recalled that the emperor Theodosius in the previous year had issued his decree *Cunctos populos* which made orthodox Christianity the religion of the empire and specified that the religion in question, if Catholics had any doubt, was that practiced by Damasus of Rome and Peter of Alexandria. Hence the reference to "rights of communon flowing from Rome." As some have noted, when you want the government to do something for you, speak to them in their own terms.

There is no question then that Ambrose honored the Roman see, but there are other texts which seem to establish a certain distance and independence as well. He commented, for example, that Peter's primacy was a primacy of confession, not of honor; a primacy of faith, not rank (*De incarnationis Domini sacramento* 32).[6] The church of Milan had a special predilection for the ceremony of foot-washing. "We are not unaware of the fact that the church in Rome does not have this custom, whose character and form we follow in all things. Yet it does not have the custom of washing the feet ... In all things I desire to follow the church in Rome, yet we too have human minds" (*De sacramentis* III.1.5).[7]

Finally, one further text should be mentioned in connection with Ambrose since it is a text which like *Roma locuta est* has become something of a shibboleth or slogan. This is the brief phrase from his commentary on the fortieth psalm: *Ubi Petrus, ibi ecclesia.*[8] During the uproar following the publication of *Humanae vitae* by Paul VI in July 1968, Cardinal Cooke of New York is reported to have signalled his loyalty by telegraphing these words to Rome.

But, as Roger Gryson has shown, in his study on Ambrose and the priesthood, the context of such a statement has nothing to do with any treatise on ecclesiology. It is but one statement in a long chain of allegorical exegesis starting with the line from Ps. 41.9: "Even my bosom friend in whom I trusted ... has lifted his heel against me."

This is not to deny the fairly common association of Peter as the symbol of the Church, the *figura ecclesiae* we have seen in Augustine. But it says little that is new and nothing at all about papal authority. Ambrose then, like others, honors the Roman church, sees it as the center of communion for the Church, or at least for the Western Church, but does not hesitate to differ from it on certain issues when he sees fit to do so.

Jerome

Jerome[9] is *sui generis*. The great Father is not known for theology but is the representative Scripture scholar of Christian Antiquity. He is the only great Father who was not a bishop. He was ordained a priest by Paulinus of Antioch, leader of the small dissident group supported by the West, a few years before John Chrysostom was ordained a deacon by Meletius, the leader of the larger orthodox group in Antioch supported by Easterners such as Basil. Yet Jerome never functioned as a priest and apparently never had any intention of doing so to the point that when his monastery in Bethlehem needed the services of a priest, he did not volunteer but forced his younger brother, Paulinianus, to be ordained by Epiphanius. Jerome then is best seen as the exemplar of the scholar-monk.

He was born in what is now northern Yugoslavia at Strido whose precise location is unknown. He is associated primarily with places in Italy such as Aquileia and especially with Rome where he studies as a young man. After a somewhat dissolute student life, he was baptized in Rome and thereafter considered himself a Roman Christian. He sought to lead the life of a monk in various locations, East and West. At that time, *conversio* meant for many who had been brought up as Christians but not baptized, not just accepting baptism but leaving the world to lead the life of a hermit or monk.

When dealing with Jerome, a further factor that must be kept in mind is his rhetoric. His style is typical of the age, yes, but it is more exaggerated than usual, even for the fourth-fifth centuries. Indeed, some modern authors have claimed that

Jerome should be considered among the great satirists of Latin literature. In an early sojourn in the Syrian desert among eastern monks, Jerome found himself frequently engaged in controversy with those around him on Trinitarian questions. This in turn usually involved the confusion caused by differences in Latin and Greek (not to mention Syriac!) conceptions and language. He wrote two letters to Pope Damasus asking for guidance, letters framed in the most fawning terms. In these letters, language commonly used for the Church as a whole was now used by Jerome of the see of Peter. "On that rock I know the Church is built. Whoever shall eat the lamb outside this house is profane. If any be not with Noah in the ark, he shall perish in the flood" (*Ep.* 15.2).[10] He goes on to tell Damasus that whatever he may declare to be the faith will be the Gospel for Jerome, three hypostases or one, even a new creed to replace that of Nicaea. In the context of the time, these are rather wild words but they are illustrative of Jerome's manner of writing. It has been said that among Jerome's chief characteristics were an inability to stay out of controversy and a grovelling manner in the presence of authority.

While we know of no response to Jerome from Rome nor can we even be sure Damasus ever saw these early letters, in fact, a few years later, Jerome, now back in Rome, became Damasus' secretary for the last two years of the Pope's life. Hence the traditional but anachronistic depiction of Jerome as a cardinal. He even tells us modestly that he might have been chosen Damasus' successor in 384 though we cannot be sure if anyone else shared these sentiments. It was this brief stay in Rome that launched Jerome on the work for which he is chiefly remembered, the revision of the Old Latin text of Scripture. Because of controversy in Rome, he soon returned to the East where he spent the rest of his life in his monastery in Bethlehem, supported financially by Paula.

In the end, he did not have all that much to say about the position of Rome, and what he did say is to some extent vitiated by his habitual exaggeration. For example, at times, he repeated that Pauline praise of the faith of the Romans (e.g., Gal II Preface; *Adv. Jovin* II.37-8).[11] He attacked his erstwhile friend Rufinus of Aquileia for translating Origen's

De principiis into Latin. In his letter praising his late disciple
Marcella, he implied not only that Origenism was a threat to
the purity of the faith of the Romans but that it had succeeded
in gaining a foothold: "... the muddy feet of heretics fouled
the clear waters of the faith of Rome..." (*Ep.* 127.9).

V

"Speak for Yourself":
The Roman View

The troubles of the time of Constantius II and his efforts to impose his own dubious views on the western Church were still having tragic results in Rome. After Liberius returned to Rome from exile somewhat under a cloud, he carried on quietly for the rest of his episcopate even as his erstwhile replacement, Felix, lingered on peacefully in the suburbs until his death in November 365. The Roman community apparently could live divided between two bishops for a while, but with the death of Liberius in September of 366, this peace was rudely shattered by the violent campaign to choose a successor. Damasus[1] was supported by the patrons of Felix while a fellow deacon of Damasus, Ursinus, found support among those followers of Liberius who thought Damasus disloyal. Damasus was ordained bishop on October 1 in the Lateran basilica, but violent confrontations between rival groups continued throughout the month of October. Late in that month, 137 followers of Ursinus were killed in what is now the church of Saint Mary Major.

The pagan historian Ammianus Marcellinus, generally fair and even-handed in his occasional passing remarks about Christianity, wrote:

> I do not deny, when I consider the ostentation that reigns at Rome, that those who desire such rank and power may be justified in laboring with all possible exertion and vehemence

* Notes for this chapter can be found on pp. 159-61

to obtain their wishes; since, after they have succeeded, they will be free from care for the future, being enriched by offerings from matrons and feasting luxuriously, so that their entertainments surpass even royal banquets. And they might be really happy if, despising the vastness of the city, behind which they hide their faults, they were to live in imitation of some of the bishops in the provinces, whom the most rigid abstinence in eating and drinking, plainness of apparel, and eyes always cast on the ground, recommend to the everlasting Deity and his true worshippers as pure and reverent men (*Res gestae* XXVII.3.14-15).[2]

Damasus, who had earlier been known as the *matronarum auriscalpius,* "the ladies' ear tickler," had many charges brought against him in court by his enemies, including charges of murder and adultery.

But lest we jump to conclusions too quickly, we might do well to recall the words of Gregory Nazianzus (*Oration* 42.24)[3] when he resigned as bishop of Constantinople in 381. He noted with considerable sarcasm that probably his tastes were not rich enough or his life-style sufficiently opulent to qualify him to be bishop of the imperial city. "I did not know that we ought to ride on splendid horses and drive in magnificent carriages and be preceded by a procession and surrounded by applause, etc. . . . " Thus it seems that the bishop of an imperial city, be it Rome or Constantinople, like it or not, found himself in a situation requiring considerable display and expenditure. We should not exaggerate, however. The monumental study of Charles Pietri, *Roma Christiana,* has found that while the Roman church was rich at this time, the wealthiest Roman families were richer still.

This gives some idea of the state of the Roman church within. What about its position in the world Church? How did it present itself to other churches in East and West? Once the testimony of Rome's self-image began to be expressed, it was strong and clear. In reaction presumably to the third canon of the Council of Constantinople in 381 which asserted the rights of Constantinople as New Rome to be second after old Rome, the Roman council of 382[4] declared that the authority of the

Roman church was not derived from conciliar decisions of the past but was based on the words of the Lord, "Thou are Peter, etc." Further, the second and third sees in the Church were listed as well. Alexandria and Antioch were there because they were also Petrine sees. Peter taught for a time in Antioch and Peter's disciple, Mark, was the evangelist of Alexandria. Thus, by this criterion, there was no room at the top for that non-apostolic upstart, Constantinople.

So was born Rome's Petrine theory. For the West with its one church of apostolic origin, there was now a means of granting an order of precedence to a few of the many Eastern sees of apostolic origin. The criterion was their connection with Peter. This both preserved Roman supremacy and excluded Constantinople. The system remained monarchical but allotted important though subordinate status to the ancient sees in the East. The Eastern preferred view, the so-called Pentarchical theory, that the universal Church was to be guided by the five principal sees, including Constantinople and Jerusalem, in some sort of conciliar way, was typically collegial rather than monarchical.

On the contrary, it was the monarchical Roman view that its decision spelled the ultimate criterion for the acceptance or rejection of councils.[5] The council of Ariminum of 359, which had crowned Constantius' drive to enforce his views on the West, had assembled a large number of bishops but since the Roman church had neither been represented nor had it accepted (received) it, it was null and void (Siricius, *ep.* 1.2; Damasus, *ep.* 1). On the other hand, the council of Nicaea and its decisions (which Damasus had unhistorically claimed was directed by the bishop of Rome - *ep.* 1) must be maintained with perpetual firmness (*Idem*). The Roman church recognized only the canons of Nicaea (Innocent, *ep.* 5, *ep.* 7.3).[6] This stance would later be exaggerated further by Leo who, in rejecting canon 28 of Chalcedon, claimed that Nicaea had forever set the order of precedence of the principal sees of Christendom: Rome, Alexandria, Antioch. It could hardly have been in a position to discuss the rank of Constantinople inasmuch as that city had not yet come into existence. This Nicene exclusivism would be further enhanced by the Roman insistence on attaching the appeal canons of Sardica to the canons of Nicaea, thus claiming the immense prestige of Nicaea for all appeals to Rome.

The Roman see was frequently consulted on a variety of questions. This reluctance of provincial bishops to see to their own problems and the propensity to seek Roman guidelines was obviously an important factor in fostering both centralization and greater uniformity of practice in the West. Such directions as Rome gave were not to be looked upon as mere advice; Roman directions were to be followed (Siricius, *ep.* 1:8.12). Refusal to obey would bring not only excommunication by Rome but the fires of Hell in the next life *(Siricius, ep.* 5.4). Heretics and blasphemers were damned in perpetuity, as Siricius put, "by divine sentence and our judgment" (*ep.* 7.4). The Roman church was the norm and authority for all the churches (Innocent, *ep.* 2.1).

Rome was never a great theological center; indeed, most of the thinking about the great theological questions of the early centuries, the Trinitarian and Christological issues, was carried on in the East. When the West was consulted about such theological issues, it usually only reacted. So when Rome wrote to other sees, especially those in the West, it was almost always a question of disciplinary issues. Victricius of Rouen, to whom Innocent addressed his second letter, was told that it was his, the local bishop's, responsibility to see to it that these Roman rules and regulations were passed on to others and came into general use. The Roman rules should become their rule-book as well (Innocent, *ep.* 2.1). This tactic was used frequently by Rome. It was the duty of those who received letters from Rome to see to it that the Roman decisions and rules were spread far and wide. So Siricius had instructed the Spanish bishop, Himerius of Tarragona, in 385. The replies given to his questions by Siricius were to be sent to all corners of the Iberian peninsula for, as he put it, "No priest of the Lord is free to be ignorant of the statutes of the Apostolic see and the venerable provisions of the canons" (Siricius, *ep.* 1.20). Innocent made similar demands of Alexander of Antioch (*ep.* 24.4.3) and commended the African bishops for consulting him in the Pelagian affair "for the good of all" (*ep.* 29).[7]

Zosimus told bishop Hesychius of Salona to spread the word to the other bishops of Illyricum.

Vigilance

The Roman see's view of its principal duty might be summed up in one word: vigilance. It must be on the lookout for deviations from the apostolic, that is, Roman, norm. Borrowing the Pauline phrase, the Roman bishop was burdened with the "care for all the churches". (2 Cor. 11:29; see e.g., Siricius, *epp.* 1.7.8; 6.1; Sixtus, *ep.* 1.6). It must always watch for those things which will destroy the unity of the churches. The less vigilant are warned to wake up, to be on the lookout for troubles. Apparently those who received the warning were regarded by Rome as aware of the problems but ignoring them. This was the case with the warning to John of Jerusalem from Pope Innocent (*ep.* 35) in the wake of the so-called "Pelagian" disturbances in the Holy Land against Jerome. Innocent praised the African bishops for being vigilant against Pelagius (*ep.* 29). The Roman role was recognized by others, as when the council of Ephesus (431) wrote to Pope Celestine (*ep.* 20.1). Victricius of Rouen (Innocent, *ep.* 2.17) and Maximian, Nestorius' successor as bishop of Constantinople, were both exhorted to increased vigilance (Celestine, *ep.* 24.3). In the wake of the Roman condemnation of Origenism, Pope Anastasius recalled his own duty of vigilance (*ep.* 1.5).[8]

Papal Vicars

The care for all the churches was not an easy task, especially given the difficulty of communications in the ancient world. Thus Rome enlisted other local churches in different regions to help in this work. The clearest, longest-standing and, for a time, most successful of these vicariates can be seen in the correspondence between successive bishops of Rome and bishops of Thessalonika. The immediate occasion for this

Roman initiative was the transferral of part of the Balkans from the jurisdiction of the western to that of the eastern emperor at the time of Theodosius I. This move would help to perpetuate Roman supremacy over the area. So, no bishops were to be ordained in the region of Illyricum without the assent of the bishop of Thessalonika (Siricius, *ep.* 4). The care for the churches of Macedonia and Achaia had been entrusted to him, Pope Boniface reminded bishop Rufus (*ep.* 4.2). Peter himself was keeping an eye on Rufus to see that he did his job well (Boniface, *ep.* 5.1). So the position of papal vicar was not an easy one. If the vicar did not do enough, Rome would not be happy. But if he were too demanding and interfered too often, the local bishops would complain directly to Rome, and Thessalonika would hear about that as well.

Upon his election, Innocent, writing to bishop Anysius of Thessalonika to renew the by-now traditional vicariate, praised his predecessors for the "complete rigor of ecclesiastical authority" with which Anastasius "had ruled the people of God" (Innocent, *ep.* 1). He worked to clear away every stain from the Church (Innocent, *ep.* 32). The papal vicar in Thessalonika was to correct such things and to gather together what had been scattered, using the authority entrusted to him by the apostolic see (Boniface, *ep.* 5.2). Similar terms were used by Celestine when writing to Cyril of Alexandria concerning the case of Nestorius (Celestine, *ep.* 11; *ep.* 14.7 to the people of Constantinople.).[9]

To the Roman delegates to the council of Ephesus who would be his direct representatives there, Celestine spoke of the supreme principle which should guide their actions, namely, that the authority of the apostolic see must be maintained (*ep.* 17). If the debate arose in the council, these delegates were to put forth for the council the decisions already made by Celestine (*ep.* 18.5).

The attempt by Pope Zosimus to turn his friend, Patroclus, bishop of Arles, into a metropolitan and a kind of papal vicar for southern Gaul became a source of endless problems for his successors (Zosimus, *ep.* 1.1). The other bishops in the region did not accept the arrangement (Zosimus, *ep.* 10). But that did not stop his successor, Boniface, from extending his horizons.

Peter was entrusted with the care of the *universal* Church by the Lord's command. "This brings my attention to extend even to places in the East which came into my sight in some way because of this very concern" (Boniface, *ep.* 15.1).

Rome continued to remind its correspondents, especially in the West, that it was always to be consulted. This process was not really an effort to search out the truth, since Rome already had it. The purpose of the consultation was that it allowed the questioner either to be corrected, if wrong, or to be *confirmed* in the truth, if right (Damasus, *ep.* 10.2). Write to Rome as to the head of your body, exhorted Siricius (*ep.* 1.15.20), or as to the head of the churches (Innocent, *ep.* 17.1 to Rufus). Bishops were encouraged to ask rather than to act on their own. Innocent praised bishop Exsuperius of Toulouse who had asked for guidance from Rome rather than, as the Pope put it, do what seemed best to him with "presumptuous usurpation" (Innocent, *ep.* 6).

In theory, only selected cases were to be directed to Rome (Boniface, *ep.* 5.4). A more canonical way of expressing Rome's wish was this: major cases were to be sent on to the apostolic see (e.g., Innocent, *ep.* 2.5).[10] But woe to the vicar who judged a major case a minor one. Then as now many a bishop deemed it the wiser course to send *all* cases to Rome. After all, as Innocent told the African bishops in his reply concerning the case of Pelagius, no case could be considered ended until it had come to the attention of the Roman see.

> Why did you affirm it by your action if you did not know that replies always flow from the apostolic font to petitioners in all the provinces? In particular, I think that as often as an argument on the faith is being blown about, all our brother and fellow bishops ought to refer it solely to Peter, that is, to the one having the authority of his name and rank, as your Charity has now done, so that it may be for the common benefit of all the churches (*ep.* 30).

Questions were thus welcomed. Zosimus expressed amazement that bishop Hesychius of Salona had never heard of a certain Roman ruling. If he had any doubts about his authority to take certain steps, no need to be concerned, Rome would supply for anything lacking (Zosimus, *ep.* 9.1-2). On another occasion, Innocent, after receiving one request, wondered out loud how anyone could ask such a stupid question, but he did not neglect to answer it anyway (Innocent, *ep.* 37.1-2 to bishop Felix of Nucerius).

This was perfectly correct procedure in the Roman view. Peter had been elevated to the summit of the priesthood by the Lord himself (Boniface, *ep.* 4.1).[11] The bishop of Rome was the head and peak of the episcopate (Innocent, *ep.* 37.1). What a Roman decision accomplished was to strengthen, to confirm a view or a decision taken by another local church or council. Thus the frequent use in this correspondence of words like *firmare* and its cognates. This "glorious Peter, prince of the Apostles," had confirmed the Roman church with his faith (Anastasius, *ep.* 2.2). Or, as Innocent assured the African bishops:

> Because it has been decreed by a divine, not a human authority, that whenever action is taken in any of the provinces, however distant or remote, it should not be brought to a conclusion before it comes to the knowledge of this see, so that every decision may be affirmed by our authority (*ep.* 29.1; cf. also Zosimus, *ep.* 15.1; Celestine, *ep.* 13.9)

The tone of command is all-pervasive. If you do not obey, you will be "plucked from the solid apostolic rock upon which Christ built the universal Church" (Siricius, *ep.* 1.2.3). Every body is ruled by its head, argued Sixtus III (*ep.* 10.4), and this head must be respected and honored. The eyes must keep a close watch on the body. But if the body does not support the head, it soon loses its firmness and vigor. All have at one time or another sought the views and approval of the Roman see, even as Gelasius would strongly stress later on, the greatest sees and bishops of the East, Athanasius and Peter of Alexandria, Meletius and Flavian of Antioch among them (Boniface, *ep.* 15.6).[12]

The final touch to the claim of supreme authority was added

by Zosimus and Boniface in the early fifth century. Ironically it was the letter to the African bishops in which Zosimus backed away from his seeming approval of Pelagius and Celestius after the harsh reaction it stirred up. But he wrote in *ep.* 12.1:

> Although the tradition of the Fathers has assigned such great authority to the apostolic see that no one would dare to dispute its judgment, and has kept this always by canons and rules and church order, and in the current of its laws pays the reverence which it owes to the name of Peter, from whom it descends.... His place we rule and we inherit the power of his name; you know this, dearest brothers, and as priests you ought to know it. Such then being our authority, that no one can revise our sentence, we have done nothing etc....

Shortly thereafter Boniface made similar statments, writing to Rufus (*ep.* 13.2), "For it has never been lawful to reconsider what has once been settled by the apostolic see," and in *ep.* 15.5 also to Rufus, "None has ever been so rash as to oppose the apostolic primacy, the judgment of which may not be revised; no one rebels against it unless he would be judged in his turn."

What is the basis for such claims? It all goes back to Peter. Borrowing perhaps the Cyprianic metaphor (*ep.* 59.14), Pope Siricius, writing to the African bishops, reminded them on the occasion of a Roman council assembled in St. Peter's basilica around the remains of the Apostle, that both the apostolate and the episcopate take their origins from Peter (*ep.* 5.1; this is repeated by Innocent in his letter to Victricius, *ep.* 2.2).[13] Another letter of Innocent (*ep.* 29.1), also to the African bishops on the occasion of their anti-Pelagian council, gives a variation on the theme: "...all of us who are placed in this position desire to follow the Apostle himself, from whom the very episcopate and whole authority of its name are derived."

As noted above, in the Roman view, other sees have significance, not because of their civic or historical eminence, but because of their relationship to Peter. This is especially true for

Antioch (Innocent, *epp.* 23, 24.1). The sixth canon of Nicaea which allotted what might be termed "spheres of influence" to Rome, Alexandria and Antioch, was based not on the importance of a city, claimed the Roman view, but on the fact that Antioch was the first see of the first of the Apostles.

Peter's Continuing Presence

More mysteriously, there was not simply an historical link to Peter growing more tenuous with each successive Roman bishop, but somehow, as they came to see it, Peter himself continued to rule and act in each man. It was Peter who showed each pope how the office was to be exercised (Damasus, *ep.* 7). Many years before, the letter of the council of Arles to Pope Sylvester (314) had expressed similar conceptions: "but since you were by no means able to leave that region where the Apostles daily sit and their blood without ceasing bears witness to the glory of God...."[14]

Later popes developed the theme as did Siricius in his letter to Himerius: "We bear the burden of all who are heavily laden or, rather, the blessed Apostle Peter bears them in us, who in all things, as we trust, protects and defends those who are heirs of his government" (*ep.* 1.1). In his exhortation to Rufus his vicar in Thessalonika, Boniface warned him that "the most blessed Apostle Peter watches with his eyes in what manner you exercise the office of rector." "He who was appointed shepherd of the Lord's sheep in perpetuity cannot but be very close to you, cannot but watch over any church, no matter where it is situated..." (Boniface, *ep.* 5.1). Since Peter is the *janitor caeli,* the "gate-keeper of Heaven," anyone disagreeing with him may well be concerned about his own eternal dwelling place (Boniface, *ep.* 15.4). Sometimes the papal actions are simply termed Peter's actions. So, Innocent condemns "with apostolic mouth" (*ep.* 17.7.14) and Boniface states that Perigenes had been confirmed as bishop of Corinth by the Apostle Peter at the instigation of the Holy Spirit (*ep.* 15.7). The Apostle Peter still has the care of all so that a pope cannot excuse himself from his duty (Celestine to the council of

Ephesus, *ep.* 22.6). The various popes or Peter in each of them always faithfully handed on what he had received (Sixtus III, *ep.* 6.5).[15]

Apostolic Uniformity?

This great self-confidence that Rome was always to be the final arbiter for disputed questions and the ultimate watchman whose vigilance guarded against corruption was not based solely either on the continuing presence of Peter or on the Lord's historical commission to Peter. The Apostles had not just bequeathed general guidelines to the Church. In a profoundly unhistorical view, the Apostles were believed to have decided everything down to small details, not just in doctrine, but also in liturgy and general practice. A basic premise was that the Roman church alone had faithfully and unerringly kept these traditions unsullied and unaltered. The Roman church keeps the old rules handed down by the Apostles or by apostolic men (Innocent, *ep.* 17.5.9).[16] The classic expression of this mentality can be found in the letter of Pope Innocent to a bishop in central Italy, bishop Decentius of Gubbio. This letter has usually been studied for its significance for the history of liturgy.

> 1. If the priests of the Lord wished to preserve intact the ecclesiastical institutions as they were handed down by the blessed Apostles, no diversity or variety would obtain in the ordinances or consecrations. But when one decides that something is to be observed simply because it has appealed to him rather than because it has been legitimately handed down, a diversity appears to be transmitted and honored in different churches and places. It all becomes a scandal to the laity who, because they do not know that the ancient traditions had been corrupted by human presumption, might think that the churches are out of communion with each other or that disagreement had been introduced by the Apostles and their associates.
>
> 2. Who does not know or reflect that that which has been handed down by Peter, the chief of the Apostles, to the

Roman church and is even now kept, must be honored by all, and that nothing ought to be imposed or introduced which has no authority, or seems to derive its precedents elsewhere? - especially since it is obvious that in all Italy, Gaul, Spain, Africa and Sicily and the adjacent islands, no one founded any churches except those which the venerable Apostle Peter or his successors established. Let these people read whether in their provinces any other of the Apostles is found or if tradition records any of them as having taught there. If they cannot read it because they can find it nowhere, it is necessary for them to follow what the Roman church observes, from which they undoubtedly first received them, lest while they are eager for foreign declarations, they seem to neglect the source of their institutions (*ep.* 25).[17]

Following Innocent's suggestion about the Roman origins of every western church, Pope Zosimus tried to support his client in Arles by an "historical" appeal to one Trophimus, sent by Peter to evangelize Gaul, and the first bishop of Arles (*ep.* 1.3, 2). [He was probably a bishop in the third century.] All Gaul received the faith through him. Thus any Gallic bishop refusing to defer to bishop Patroclus of Arles was going against not only the apostolic see but also against ancient customs and the reverence due to Trophimus (*ep.* 6.1-2). Those in Gaul who did not respect the authority of Arles were the innovators because "with us, antiquity lives on, its roots undisturbed" (Zosimus, *ep.* 5). Scripture must be interpreted according to the tradition of the Fathers and the ancestors (*ep.* 2.8). Because of the Roman fidelity to Peter and the apostolic traditions, "From this fountain, the peace of the faith of Catholic brotherhood is sent unclouded into the whole world" (*ep.* 2.1).

Given the emphasis on tradition, novelty—and we are still dealing here primarily with discipline—was a bad word. If things are now done differently elsewhere from the way Rome still does them, then novelty has been introduced and it must stop (Boniface, *ep.* 14.2, 4). Writing to Rufus, Innocent stresses that he is proposing nothing new; Rufus should simply carry on as before (Innocent, *ep.* 13.2). Laziness and neglect have led to deviations. bishops must be on their guard against this (Vigilance!). But even if others are not, Rome never slackens its vigilance. Neglect of rules may be a threat to concord in faith (Innocent, *ep*. 3 to Toledo; Siricius, *ep*. 5.1).[18] "Let not some new commandments be ordered, but let us wish that those things which through the sloth of certain people have been neglected, may now be observed by all, those things which have been instituted by the tradition of the Apostles and the Fathers . . ."(Innocent, *ep*. 2.2). These unhappy deviations can be remedied by returning to the Roman norm, as in the case of the ritual which bishop Decentius was invited to come to Rome to see and then by all means to return home to Gubbio to implement to the letter (Innocent, *ep*. 25; Celestine, *ep*. 4.5).

Another threat to tradition was the danger of caving in to popular whims and passing fads. Celestine put it most bluntly: "The people are to be taught, not followed"(*ep*. 5.3), a lesson Gelasius would clearly extend to the emperor himself. We must not permit ourselves to keep silence on matters in which our silence will give rise to the assumption that we support certain things we should not support. Rather we must teach the people the correct discipline (Innocent, *ep*. 2.2).

We have no choice. "The rules rule us; we do not stand over the rules; let us be subject to the canons . . ."(Celestine, *ep*. 3). With such views, it is no surprise that the Roman bishops frequently expressed the idea that they were bound by the decisions of their predecessors. Similar ideas go back quite a way, for example, to the Quartodeciman controversy. Polycarp failed to persuade bishop Anicetus "to observe it, for he said he ought to keep the custom of those who were presbyters before him"(Eusebius, *H. E.* V.24.16). A little later there is the report from Tertullian in his *Adversus Praxean* that a bishop of Rome, about to recognize or show some form of favor to the Montanist movement in Asia Minor, was dissuaded from doing so by Praxeas, "by insisting on the decisions of the bishop's predecessors."[19] All the way to *Humanae Vitae* of 1968 and beyond no doubt, this principle is still a living, working basis in Rome. All we have looked at supports this basic operating principle of the Roman bishops. Innocent, writing to Anysius of Thessalonika, expressed his intention to carry on the tradition of his predecessors going back to Damasus. "It would not be right for me to go against the judgment of so many great men in whose place I have succeeded . . . " (*ep.* 1).

To preserve the unity of the Church, all must be in harmony, all must speak the same language (Innocent, *ep.* 14; Sixtus, *ep.* 1.2). To do this, they must not depart from the traditions of the Fathers (Celestine, *ep.* 14.2). Even the emperor must do his part to ensure orthodoxy; if he does, God will bless the empire (Celestine, *ep.* 19.2). [Celestine can still say this after all that had happened to the empire!]

We have often heard that the Roman church, while insistent on unity of doctrine, is very open about variety of rites and differing customs, liturgies, and the like. The early Popes do not bear this out. All facets of Church life are intimately bound together. "If there is one faith, there must remain as well one tradition; if there is one tradition, one discipline must be observed throughout the whole Church" (Damasus, *ep.* 10 to the bishops of Gaul).

> Dearest brother, if this rule is observed by all God's bishops with complete vigilance, ambition will cease, dissent will grow quiet, heresies and schisms will not emerge, the devil will find no opportunity to run amok, unanimity will remain, iniquity, overcome, will be trampled upon, the truth will flame out in spiritual fire, peace, preached now with the lips, will be in accord with the will of the soul (Innocent, *ep.* 2.17).[20]

In the view of the Roman bishops from Damasus to Sixtus, unity must be a uniformity with Roman ways since Rome alone has always without deviation observed and preserved the apostolic traditions. There is no room for differences. *Obsta principiis.* Stop things before they can get going, before they can take root. If you give an inch, people will take a mile. Therefore, do not give an inch. Such are the axioms of the classical mindset which does not recognize the reality of change except as degeneration from a primitive ideal. How little has changed over the centuries, except that more and more, with the passage of time, Rome has succeeded in imposing the kind of centralization and uniformity that antiquity could only long for as its ideal.

VI

Two Styles of Leadership: Leo and Gelasius

Leo the Great (440-461)

The pontificate of Leo I[1] has traditionally been viewed as the high point of the ancient papacy. His theology of the Church and his own place in it as bishop of Rome are not radically different from or more advanced than those of his recent predecessors. There was no fundamental breakthrough or escalation. The first few years of his tenure were dominated by problems from the past, largely disciplinary in nature and western in origin. For example, the position of Arles among the churches of southern Gaul continued to be a sore point, heightened by the persistence of the bishop of that time, Hilary. Yet there are differences from the past as well. With Leo for the first time we have literary remains other than letters, that is, a number of sermons. These help us to get an idea of Leo as theologian and pastor. And his sense of liturgical time is impressive.

But then comes a significant change. From about 448 on, his time and thoughts are dominated by the Christological problem in the East: Eutyches, the "robber council" of 449 at Ephesus, the effort to persuade the emperor to call a new council, the council of Chalcedon in 451 and the growing opposition to that council in some parts of the East in his last decade as Pope. In a sense this overriding controversy distorts

* Notes for this chapter can be found on pp. 161-63

the total picture of Leo's work and unavoidably makes it different from the pontificates of his predecessors.

Leo's theological view of his office is perhaps best sought in his sermons, especially those preached on the anniversary of his episcopal ordination and on the feast of SS. Peter and Paul (June 29). Each bishop rules over the people entrusted to his care, "yet Peter especially rules all whom Christ also ruled originally" (*Sermo* 4.2). Rome, through Peter and Paul, has become "the head of the world," (*Sermo* 82.1)[2] and attained a wider sway than the historical Roman empire ever did. Peter and Paul indeed have become the twin founders of a new Rome, Christian Rome, far superior morally to the traditional fratricidal founders of ancient Rome, Romulus and Remus (*Idem*). The Apostles came to Rome because of its importance and centrality, ". . .that the light of truth which was being displayed for the salvation of all the nations might spread itself more effectively throughout the body of the world from the head itself" (*Sermo* 82.3).

Peter as the rock gives strength to the Church's faith. He confessed the divinity of Christ ". . .that in preparation for ruling the whole Church he might first learn what he would have to teach, and for the solidification of the faith which he was destined to preach, might receive the answer, 'Thou art Peter, etc.'" (*Sermo* 62.2). The firmness added by the rocklike quality of the Roman faith and decisions is a common theme in Leo. While each bishop is responsible for his flock, Leo and every bishop of Rome are responsible for all.

> We have a duty which is shared with all; in fact the function of each one is a part of our work; so that when people resort to the see of the blessed Apostle Peter from the whole world, and seek from our stewardship that love of the whole Church entrusted to him by the Lord, the greater our duty to the whole, the heavier we feel the burden to rest on us (*Sermo* 5.2).

But, as with Siricius, the burden is eased because Peter still presides in his see (*Sermo* 5.4). The power, he says, "even in our own time . . . is to be ascribed to his work and his guidance..." (*Sermo* 4.4). This common view of the Roman bishops has been appropriated by others as well. When Peter Chrysologus, bishop of Ravenna, was consulted by Eutyches from Constantinople, a sign that easterners at least still sought the views and support of westerners other than the bishop of Rome, he was told to consult Leo "since blessed Peter who lives and presides in his own see, offers the truth of the faith to those who ask. For we, in our zeal for peace and faith, cannot decide questions of faith apart from the consent of the bishop of Rome" (Leo, *ep.* 25.2).[3]

Leo does add some significant new nuances to this traditional doctrine. He takes up the Cyprianic challenge. Yes, he agrees, Peter was equal in honor to all the other Apostles (*similitudo honoris*); nevertheless there is a *discretio potestatis*; all do not have the same power (*ep.* 14.11):

> Although they were all equal in being chosen, one was allowed to stand out above the others. From this arrangement there arose, also, distinctions among the bishops. And through a vast hierarchy it was provided that everyone might not arrogate everything to himself, but particular bishops were to be set up in each province, whose opinion among the brothers was to be considered first. Certain others, again, were to assume a greater pastoral responsibility in the larger cities. And through them the care of the universal Church was to converge in the one see of Peter, and nothing was ever to be at odds with his leadership.

The hierarchical pattern is completed by the single supreme leader at the top of the pyramid. Later centuries would elaborate on this vision and distinction between the power of orders and jurisdiction.

But he goes further. For Cyprian, Peter received the power from Christ first in order to symbolize unity. Leo does not deny this, but he stresses the significance of the fact that the other Apostles received their power *through* Peter.

> The right of this power (that is, of the keys) did indeed pass on to the other apostles, and the order of this decree passed

on to all the chiefs of the Church; but not in vain was that which was imparted to all entrusted to one. Therefore this is commended to Peter separately, because all the rulers of the Church are invested with the figure of Peter. The privilege therefore of Peter remains, wherever judgment is passed from his equity. . . . So then in Peter the strength of all is fortified, and the help of divine grace is so ordered that the stability which through Christ is given to Peter, through Peter is conveyed to the Apostles (*s.* 4.3).[4]

Throughout Leo's vision of the Church, then, Peter and his successors are the leaders of the Church.

Like his predecessors, Leo commissioned the bishop of Thessalonika, Anastasius at this period, to be his vicar for the lower Balkan area (*ep.* 6.2). The vicar handles the minor cases, passing on the more important affairs to Rome (*ep.* 5.6). He keeps a vigilant eye on things to be sure that discipline and tradition are being observed. Leo is to be kept informed so that he may do his duty of being vigilant and solicitous for the welfare of the whole Church (*ep.* 6.1). Leo wrote as well to the bishops of the area to remind them both of his own duty of vigilance and of their duty to respect the bishop of Thessalonika because Peter's primacy among the Apostles means that Leo's pastoral duty extends through all the Church (*ep.* 5.2).

Anastasius apparently showed an excessive amount of zeal so that other bishops complained directly to Leo, who lamented that he was being blamed for Anastasius' imprudence (*ep.* 14.1). Anastasius was exhorted to imitate Leo's moderation and kindness (*Idem;* cf. *s.* 5.5). Leo's ministry is supposed to be of service rather than of presiding. This letter contains an expression that would have a great future. Leo reminded Anastasius that he should not be carried away. He only shared a part of Leo's pastoral responsibility; he did not possess the *plenitudo potestatis* (*ep.* 14.1).

Papal Activity in the West

Leo's correspondence with western, that is, Italian and

Gallic, bishops, both before and during the Chalcedonian crisis, is similar to that of his predecessors. Writing to the bishops of Campania in 443, he reminded them of his duty of vigilance against laxity of discipline and went on to complain about those being ordained, usury, and other practical problems. Anyone violating previous discipline will be removed from office (*ep.* 4.5).[5] In 447, he objected that the bishops of Sicily were departing from the traditional dates for baptism. This would never have happened, he observed, "if the see of the blessed Peter the Apostle, which is the mother of your priestly dignity, were also your teacher in ecclesiastical procedure" (*ep.* 16.1). They should come to the Roman council to learn. "We lay it to your Charities' charge not to deviate at all in future from customs initiated by the Apostles. For, hereafter, no one can be excused if he believes that apostolic regulations can be neglected in any way" (*ep.* 16.7).

To the bishops of the province of Vienne in Gaul, he wrote to warn that those who separated themselves from the "solidity of Peter no longer were part of the Church," or, as he put it, "no longer shared in the divine mystery" (*ep.* 10.1). Roman persistence in urging its own point of view bore fruit when later letters from the Gallic bishops to Rome echoed the Roman descriptions of Peter's position.

> ...Standing as it were on the watchtower of love with apostolic care and watchfulness, you (Leo) cry aloud, lest the enemy come upon us unawares ... Moreover, we, who specially belong to you, are filled with a great and unspeakable delight because this special statement of your teaching is so highly regarded wherever the churches meet together, that the unanimous opinion is expressed that the primacy of the Apostolic see is rightfully there assigned, whence the oracles of the Apostolic Spirit still receive their interpretation (*ep.* 68.1).

A few years later, other bishops from Gaul, led by Ravennius of Arles, wrote to express their acceptance of and appreciation for, Leo's *Tome,* "to the apostolic see, whence flowed out the fountain and origin of our religion" (*ep.* 99.5).[6]

Yet, despite the respect, the embers of conflict every so often flamed up again. Arles was one such tinderbox. Zosimus had laid the groundwork for a long-running headache for the popes. If Roman rhetoric could be sent back to Rome by Gallic bishops, so could Roman arguments. So *circa* 450, the bishops of the province of Arles wrote to Leo to support the restoration of metropolitan rights to the bishop of Arles. They cited the alleged mission of Trophimus brought forward by Zosimus back at Rome: ". . . believing it to be fully reasonable and just that, just as through the most blessed Peter, prince of the Apostles, the most holy Roman Church holds the chief positio (*principatus*) above all the churches of the entire world, so also, in Gaul, the church of Arles, which merited to have as bishop St. Trophimus, sent by the Apostles, should have the right of ordaining bishops" (*ep.* 65.2).

Roman Dealings with the East

As always, dealings with the East are more difficult to evaluate. The council of Ephesus of 449 under the leadership and largely under the control of Dioscuros of Alexandria, boldly suppressed Leo's *Tome.* He would not even allow it to be read despite Leo's claim in his letter to the council that the emperor had "wished the authority of the Apostolic see to effect a settlement" (*ep.* 33.1).

In his efforts to have Ephesus II reversed, Leo enlisted members of the western imperial family and court, including the fainéant emperor, Valentinian III and his more noteworthy mother, Galla Placidia. In writing to their eastern cousins, both insisted on Roman ecclesiastical authority and used a vocabulary similar to Leo's. For example, Galla spoke of *principatus sacerdotii* and Valentinian of the *principatus episcopatus* (*epp.* 55-56).

The leading theologian of the school of Antioch, Theodoret of Cyrrhus, had been condemned by the second council of Ephesus. He petitioned Leo for redress. In his affirmative reply, Leo did not hesitate to assert Roman claims. "The rays of the Sun of Righteousness which were obscured throughout

the East by the clouds of Nestorius and Eutyches, have shone
out brightly from the West, where it has reached its zenith in
the Apostles and teachers of the Church" (*ep.* 120.2). The
Christological solution was first formulated by the foremost
see of Christendom (Leo's *Tome*) and was then received by the
judgment of the whole Christian world (*ep.* 120.1).[7]

After the council, writing to bishop Maximus of Antioch
(453), Leo reminded him of the Roman view that Antioch was
of significance because it was Peter's first see. He further
pointed out that his (Leo's) rejection of canon 28 was an
action taken on behalf of Antioch as much as of Rome. "Although at times, bishops are of different merits, the rights of
the sees remain" (*ep.* 119.3). In a letter to the emperor the next
year, he even coined an unusual expression. He urged him to
explain Leo's *Tome* to the dissident in order that they too
"may be proved sincere disciples of the apostolic see" (*ep.*
130.3).

Having taken a general look at Leo's view of Roman
primacy, we now turn to take a closer look at certain aspects
of it. First, Leo continues the Roman view that the bishop of
Rome has a true solicitude for all the churches. As he informed
the bishops of Illyricum, his *cura* extended to all (*ep.* 5.2).
". . . Who (is) so ignorant or grudging (as to) estimate the
honor of the blessed Peter so as not to believe that all parts of
the Church are ruled by his care and enriched by his help"
(*sermo* 5.4). He recalled this obligation when writing far afield
to bishops in Mauretania Caesariensis, for example (*ep.* 12.1),[8]
or to archimandrites in Constantinople against Eutyches (*epp.*
61.1; 75.1); to monks in Palestine (*ep.* 124.1) or to the Augusta
Eudokia (*ep.* 123.1) to chide them for their continuing opposition to Chalcedon. He refers to it again in an effort to
recruit Theodoret to supply him with information about the
state of the Church in his part of the world, specifically about
the strength of resistance to the council (*ep.* 120.6).

Solidity Means Irreversibility

A good part of Rome's service to the Church is to be the

guarantor of the solidity, certainty and clarity of the faith. The
see of Peter the rock is the obvious place where the faith is
strengthened. "For the solidity of the faith which was praised
in the prince of the Apostles, does not fall" (*sermo* 3.2, 3). It is
in his successors: "For their stability which the rock himself
was given by that Rock, Christ, he conveyed also to his successors, and wheresoever any steadfastness is apparent, there
without doubt is to be seen the strength of the shepherd"
(*sermo* 5.4). Notice that Leo does not deny that Christ is the
primary referent for the rock as symbol but he emphasizes all
the more the dignity of Peter who was deemed worthy to share
this quality with the Lord. He has Christ say to Peter: "Although I am the indestructible rock and the cornerstone . . .
you, too, you are the rock for my power strengthens you so
that that which I am by my own power will be held in common
by you as well by participation" (*sermo* 83.1). Fear was common to all the Apostles, but "the Lord had a special concern
for Peter and prayed especially for Peter's faith as if the others
would be more secure if the soul of the chief was not overcome." The courage of Peter is strengthened so that the *firmitas*
given to Peter by Christ may be passed on to the others
through Peter (*sermo* 83.3).

To participate in this special strength, local or regional decisions should be forwarded to Rome for confirmation (*ep.*
12.13).[9] Such was the case with the African condemnations of
Pelagius which were confirmed by Pope Innocent (*ep.* 1.2).
Conversely, if the authority of the papal vicar in Thessalonika
is ignored by local bishops, their actions, including their or-
dinations, will lack *firmitas* in the eyes of Rome (*ep.* 6.4).

In the Christological controversy, Leo consistently expressed
the concern that councils not discuss previous, firm decisions
as if there were still some possibility that such decisions could
be reversed (*ep.* 90.2). Between 449 and 451, Leo's concern
was to undo progressively the harm done at Ephesus II but
also to insure, if possible, that any new council would not
make things worse by wrangling. His tome had stated the
doctrine; it was important that the new council be united in its
consensus, as he wrote to the emperor Marcian (*ep.* 94).

When the council of Chalcedon had done its work and

Leo's hopes had been fulfilled, he wrote to the bishops in Gaul that: "The holy council has now with devoted unanimity agreed with the letter written by our humble self, a letter rightly strengthened by the authority of my master, the most blessed Apostle Peter" (*ep.* 102.4). (He repeated this view to Theodoret in 453 in *ep.* 120.5.) The *Tome* was confirmed by the judgment of the council (*ep.* 120.4) but the Apostolic See also confirmed the council (*ep.* 163).

Because of the papal rejection of canon 28, there was initially some confusion. Rumors circulated that Leo had rejected the doctrinal definitions of the council. In order to clear up the confusion, the emperor asked Leo to make a specific statement to confirm the dogmatic aspects of the council (*epp.* 116.2; 117.1). Despite his unhappiness about canon 28, Leo began to realize the threat posed to the doctrinal aspects of the council by the emergence of strong opposition in Egypt and Palestine. From the time of the death of the emperor Marcian, Leo began to urge the irreversibility of the doctrinal decisions and said much less about canon 28. It came down to this: What a council has decided and the apostolic see has confirmed is no longer open to discussion; it cannot be revised or reversed (*ep.* 160.2).[10] Such a course would be disastrous. If Chalcedon is subject to revision, so is Nicaea. "To search for what has been made clear, to go back over what has been perfectly established, to tear apart what has been defined—what else is that than to fail to return thanks for what we have received..?" (*ep.* 162.1). If Chalcedon lacks *firmitas,* so does everything else, including Nicaea (*Idem*).

Nihil Innovetur

Solicitude and responsibility for the situation in other churches requires that the one responsible be on the lookout for abuses. That awareness of responsibility we have seen in earlier bishops of Rome is still very much alive in Leo. The *episcopus* is a *speculator,* a watchman or lookout.[11] "We cannot excuse ourself to Him who wished us to be on watch if we do not repress such practices with the vigilance we should," he wrote to the bishops of Campania (*ep.* 4, prol.).[12] (Cf. also *ep.* 6.1.) The great threat to vigilance is laziness and neglect of duty. The bishop of Rome must fight against this both in himself and in other bishops (*epp.* 14.11; 16.1; 99.4).

In dealing with the troubles in the East, he tried to ensure that some sort of disciplinary actions were being taken against the perpetrators of the 449 council. He asked the emperor and empress to be careful about the choice of bishops who would be permitted to attend the next council (*ep.* 79.2 to Pulcheria). After the unforeseen death of Theodosius II in 450 and his sister's rise to power, Leo, who had been strongly urging the necessity of holding a new council, now began to doubt the wisdom of holding another council in the uncontrollable East. Now he began to ask the emperor to postpone a new council until greater security could be assured (*ep.* 83.2).[13] He warned the new bishop of Constantinople, Anatolius, to hasten reforms (*ep.* 85.1) and urged the bishop of Antioch to be more vigilant against heresy (*ep.* 119.3).

Despite the happy outcome of the council, Leo told Theodoret that this was no time to go to sleep but rather to keep working, albeit less frenetically (*ep.* 120.6). Whereas he could be direct in writing to bishops, he always had to be circumspect and sometimes indirect in addressing the emperor, especially the new emperor Leo who had succeeded Marcian. He disclaimed any attempt to dictate to him in the struggle to protect Chalcedon against its Eastern detractors. So while not dictating what the emperor was to do, Leo explained that "it is my duty to make clear what you know and to preach what you believe" (*ep.* 165.1).

Tradition made the Roman bishops fear novelty above all else. They were bound by the decisions of their predecessors, above all by the Apostles who had decided all issues and handed them on. This was the chief duty of bishops: to pass things on unchanged, intact, adding nothing and subtracting nothing. This was the fixist ideal of Antiquity. Hilary of Arles and his pretensions? Simply innovations to be rejected. Leo's ideal was not to "start something new, but to renew the old" (*non nova instituentes, sed vetera renovantes, ep.* 10.2). The classic mind is found here to the letter: to continue in the customary practices of the Fathers and in so doing to maintain order and to remove the threat of disorder (*Idem*). If the current hierarchical order is observed, there will be no dissension but only concord (*ep.* 13.1).

Problems could arise in which antiquity seems to have been violated. But if this had been done by earlier popes, nothing could be done about it now without violating the other axiom that each pope was bound by the decisions of his predecessors. This dilemma was best illustrated by the Gallic arguments over primacy. If mistakes were made in the past, they were made in the past, they were made in the name of tradition, for example, the case of Arles and Trophimus. Leo sought to restore peace through compromise, making both Arles and Vienne metropolitan sees (*ep.* 66).[14]

In the Christological controversy and in his relations with the East in general, the same denunciations of novelty were stressed. As he told the emperor Marcian, it was not permitted to depart in even one word from the Gospel and apostolic teaching (*ep.* 82.1). As he had earlier assured the Gallic bishops, that his battle against the false pretensions of Arles (*ep.* 10.9) was a battle in their interests, to protect *their* privileges, not his own, so in the furious attack against canon 28 of Chalcedon, he marshalled all the arguments against innovation, especially that his combat was an unselfish defense of Nicaea, that he was fighting for the historic rights of Alexandria and Antioch. Canon three of the council of Constantinople of 381? What kind of precedent was that? Since the apostolic see had not been informed of it, it tottered and collapsed (*ep.* 106.5).

Referring to the somewhat vague sixth canon of Nicaea which set up spheres of influence for the great sees and is at the root of the development of the system of patriarchates, Leo argued that these canons of Nicaea were now immutable (*ep.* 104.3). All would be in harmony if these canons were not tampered with (*ep.* 105.2; also, *epp.* 106.2; 115.1). In the Roman view, the three sees singled out for mention in canon 6 of Nicaea were important because they were Petrine sees. Insistence on the Nicene canons obviously left Constantinople out in the cold. Not only was it not a Petrine see, it was not even an apostolic see, although much later legends arose about

St. Andrew in Byzantium. Further it could hardly have been taken into account at Nicaea since the city did not yet exist at the time of the council in 325.

The concern with change was not just Leo's obsession. Peter himself insisted that things remain just as he left them. ". . . Peter . . . received them from that very truth which he professed" (*ep.* 119.2).[15] Stand by antiquity, Leo told the ill-fated Chalcedonian bishop Proterius of Alexandria, not just in doctrine but in discipline, too (*ep.* 129.3). In rejecting canon 28, Leo insisted that he was, with God's help, the guardian of the Catholic faith and of the ordinances of the Fathers (*ep.* 114.2). The emperors recognized this. "As was fitting for the bishop of the apostolic see, your holiness excellently saw to it that, keeping the ecclesiastical canons, nothing new was allowed in the ancient customs and order set up long ago and observed without violation to this day" (*ep.* 110). In his final struggle for the maintaining of the council of Chalcedon, the argument against novelty was still prominent. To try to call the council into question would be a great sacrilege (*ep.* 157.3). "We must dutifully and constantly make use of this already existing teaching of the Holy Spirit . . . lest the authority of divinely inspired decisions be minimized while the arguing of such men is permitted" (*ep.* 164.3).

The importance for Leo of the rule that unity of faith requires uniformity of practice is clear. As for his predecessors, the apostolic practice is still the Roman practice. Early in his pontificate, before the Christological problems came up, he wrote to Dioscuros to complain of differing customs in Alexandria. Since Mark came to Alexandria from Rome and from Peter's side, he must have taught the Alexandrian church exactly what Peter did. Why, then, except because of negligence, are there now customs in Alexandria which differ from those in Rome? "It is wrong to believe that his holy disciple Mark, who first ruled the church of Alexandria, formulated decrees with provisions other than those handed down to him" (*ep.* 9.1).[16] He would later use the same arguments against Dioscuros in the Christological controversy (*ep.* 102.4). "We cannot have it that, while admitting our membership in one body and faith, we are at variance in other matters, with some practices seemingly from the master, different ones from the disciples" (*ep.* 9.1).

Uncertainty and confusion must be eliminated. "Hence, the solicitude of the Apostolic see is ever on the watch to prevent any uncertainty from disturbing devotion in the Church" (*ep.* 138).

> But since the Spirit of Wisdom and knowledge instructed the Apostles and the teachers of the whole Church so as to allow nothing unregulated, nothing confused in Christian observance, the reasons behind the solemnities must be kept separate and well-ordered distinction must be preserved in all customs begun by the Fathers and our predecessors. For in no other way are we one flock and one shepherd unless, as the Apostle teaches, we all say the same thing and are also perfectly united in one mind and in one judgment (*ep.* 16.2).

If the church has accepted some disciplinary or devotional usage, it must come from the apostolic tradition and the instruction of the Holy Spirit (*sermo* 79.1).

Leo expressed his disgust with Dorus, bishop of Beneventum, who apparently had spent time at Rome, but now in his own see, followed different practices (*ep.* 19.1). Hence his concern, after giving instructions, always to urge that these commands be passed on to other bishops by the primary recipient. Some examples of this are: *ep.* 6.4 to Anastasius; *ep.* 159.7 to Nicetas of Aquileia and finally, *ep.* 96 to Ravennius, "so that there may be one confession of faith and one devotion in celebration."

Leo's guiding principle then is not only like that of his more recent predecessors; it hearkens further back to the letter of Clement of Rome to the Corinthians. "It is necessary that all things be in order in God's Church" (*ep.* 119.6).[17] Peter will stand for no changes, as Leo told Maximus of Antioch in 453 (*ep.* 119.2). He has strengthened the authority of Leo's *Tome* (*ep.* 102.4) and by his faith has destroyed all heresies (*ep.* 61.2). Though Leo, as every bishop of Rome, is himself an unworthy heir, Peter is still in Peter's see and still speaks (*ss.* 2.2; 3.3;4;

5.1). Peter and Paul are the two eyes of that Body of which Christ is the head (*sermo* 82.7).

Roman Authority & Conciliar Authority: Two Different Views?

Since much of Leo's pontificate was taken with the Christological problem, the question of the relationship between the role and authority of the bishop of Rome and the authority of the ecumenical council is of great significance. In an influential work, *Orient et Occident*[18] published in 1974, W. de Vries of the Oriental Institute in Rome argued forcefully that the history of each of the first seven ecumenical councils shows a clear divergence of views between East and West. Who holds the ultimate decision making power in the Church? The Papacy as in the Roman view or the ecumenical council as in the eastern view? It is clear that Rome felt not just able but compelled to reject the second council of Ephesus of 449. Then in the case of Chalcedon two years later, while happy to accept the dogmatic decision, it unequivocally rejected canon 28. As for 449, Leo reaffirmed that the protests of his legates were perfectly correct because: "What was being decided was not at all acceptable to the apostolic see" (*ep.* 44.1).[19]

According to de Vries, in the Roman view, its own decision was the definitive one; the council was not to debate it but simply to ratify it. For the East, the council took into account the Roman decision but debated the issues on its own and came to its own judgment. The decision of the council was the definitive one. Rome and the more collegial East each went on council after council with its own essentially different view. What do the texts show here?

Leo's expressions vary according to the context and the issues at stake at a given time. Before Ephesus II, he had condemned Eutyches and sent Flavian of Constantinople his tome. As he put it, the emperor "had invoked the authority of the apostolic see to effect a holy settlement" (*ep.* 33.1).[20] He then mentioned his legates for this council, stressing that they "in common with you (the other bishops at the council) (will) come to a decision that will please the Lord" (*ep.* 33.2). Such a decision clearly would have to be one in agreement with Leo's tome, not contrary to it. And so when the council turned out to be completely different, Leo rejected it quickly and totally. He kept writing to the eastern emperor and others, demanding a new council to be held in Italy, but with no result (*epp.* 44.2; 45.2; 54; 69). But when the controversy had first arisen over Eutyches, Leo had expressed the view to Flavian and to the emperor that the issue was so clear and obvious that no council was really necessary (*ep.* 36). "For the question that has arisen is not one about which there can be or ought to be any doubt" (*ep.* 37).

After the death of Theodosius II, the new imperial couple, Pulcheria and Marcian, generally in agreement with Leo, called a new council for the East. At this point, Leo, rightfully fearful of whither a new eastern council might lead, being among other things beyond his control, began to urge delay (*ep.* 73; letter of both eastern and western emperors promising a new council; *ep.* 76 from Marcian to Leo). Since Pulcheria and Marcian were determined, Leo yielded reluctantly (*epp.* 89; 90.1).

When the council began, he made it clear that he presided in the persons of his legates. "Your holinesses may consider that I am presiding at the council in these brothers ... who have been sent by the Apostolic see, and that you are not then deprived of my presence. I am now present in the person of my vicars" (*ep.* 93.1; June 26, 451). In the same letter, he also made it clear that his *Tome* presented the correct doctrine in conformity with the Scriptures (*ep.* 93.2).[21]

This part of the council went well and, as the emperors later wrote: "All agreed to the presentation, according to your Holiness' letter, as the Truth demanded" (*ep.* 100). Leo rejoiced that the Truth had triumphed and the church had been restored "in the power of the Holy Spirit acting through the services of the apostolic see" (*ep.* 104.1). More than once Leo referred to the council's agreement with his *Tome* (*ep.* 102.4). His letter "was ratified by the assent of the entire holy Synod" (*ep.* 120.4). Writing to the bishops of Gaul (*ep.* 103), he wrote that the Pope, head of the universal Church, had done it "*sancto synodo consentiente.*" Perhaps this western version tends to minimize the council's role.

There was certainly no question about Leo's rejection of Canon 28 (*epp.* 105.3; 106.5). The easterners seemed to attach a great deal of importance to obtaining Leo's approval of the canon, given the flattering terms in which they sought it. Even though they failed to obtain it, they regarded it as valid and canonical anyway. The emperor then had to ask Leo specifically to indicate his approval of the council (*ep.* 110). He finally gave it but only on March 21, 453, making it very clear that his approval extended only to the doctrinal content (*ep.* 114.1: "...*in sola videlicet causa fidei...*").

But there were more serious problems for "his" council. Defending against eastern dissidents, he emphasized that the council must not be called into question. He was also aware, after the death of the emperor Marcian, of the temptation for future emperors to attempt to reach some sort of compromise to appease the dissenters. In writing directly to the easterners, he seemed to feel that if only his *Tome* were explained more thoroughly and carefully, all objections would melt away.

Nevertheless, he held that the authority of the Pope and the council should be enough to overcome all objections and hesitations. To Palestinian monks, he wrote: "...I have laid down what we ought to think and feel on the Incarnation of the Word according to the teaching of the Gospel and apostles and in nothing have I departed from the Creed of the Holy Fathers..." (*ep.*124.1).[22] To the new emperor Leo, he felt the necessity of adding further explanations, "... although what the apostolic see has taught would suffice..." (*ep.* 156.6). To Juvenal of Jerusalem, he wrote that the *Tome* plus the confirmation of it by the council are sufficient (*ep.* 139.4), because it was done "*instruente Spiritu Sancto*" (*ep.* 144). In summary, then, as he wrote to the emperor Leo on July 10, 457: "At that council, assembled through the Holy Spirit, everything was confirmed by such complete and perfect definitions that nothing could be added or withdrawn from that arrangement, which was produced through God's direction" (*ep.* 145.1).[23]

From Leo to Gelasius

There were three popes between the death of Leo in 461 and the election of Gelasius in 492. The first, Hilary, was the papal legate who survived his manhandling at the robber council of 449. Although the eastern troubles continued, his pontificate seems like a calm interlude in which papal correspondence dealt primarily with western bishops, that is, from Italy, Gaul, and Spain, and the old themes and questions return to predominance.

Rome is the uncorrupted guardian of the tradition of the Fathers (*ep.* 4.1), seeking to win a common observance of the same discipline by all (*ep.* 6.2). Trying to establish a balance between mercy and the "vigor of apostolic discipline" (*ep.* 8.2), the Roman church was recognized by Leontius of Arles as the "mother of us all" (*ep.* 5.1). In writing to a Gallic council in 464, Hilary noted: "It has been decreed by the law of the Christian princes that whatever the High Priest of the apostolic see has deliberately appointed for the churches and their rulers, for the peace of all the Lord's priests and the observance of discipline, is to be reverently received and strictly observed . . ." (*ep.* 10.4).

This is presumably a reference to the decree of the western emperor Valentinian III against Hilary of Arles in 445 and therefore directly relevant to the situation in Gaul. I do not see it as Burn-Murdoch does as a "frank admission" (p. 257) by Pope Hilary that papal power was a direct creation of the state. The nineteenth-century Anglican author, F. W. Puller, spoke melodramatically of this imperial decree: "Thus did the decrepit autocracy of the dying empire plant in the home of freedom, the Church of God, the hateful likeness of itself" (p. 201).[24]

With the succession of Simplicius in 468, the post-Chalcedonian situation in the East came once more to the forefront of papal preoccupation. The emperor Leo died in 474. His successor, Zeno, was briefly overthrown by one Basiliscus who openly courted the Monophysites in Alexandria and their leader, the Monophysite patriarch Timothy Aelurus (+477). Even when Zeno regained the throne in 476, the temptation to compromise was growing stronger. The patriarch of Constantinople at this time was Acacius (471-489). In 482 Zeno issued the *Henoticon*, a document to promote unity, in the hopes of gaining the acceptance of the new Monophysite patriarch in Alexandria, Peter Mongos (477-490). The *Henoticon* condemned Nestorius and Eutyches, asserted that the faith is to be found in the Nicene Creed and the Twelve Anathemas of Cyril against Nestorius, but made no mention of the two natures in Christ. In other words, like many of the objectionable creeds of the fourth century, it did not openly attack the council in question (then Nicaea, now Chalcedon) but tried to slip past it in silence by ignoring it. This problem would dominate Roman concerns for a long time to come.

Pope Simplicius was always on guard against any effort in the East for compromise. This would be regarded as an attack against and betrayal of both Leo and Chalcedon, against whose teaching it is wrong to dispute (*ep.* 2.2 to Acacius). All such efforts are to be resisted (*ep.* 2.3). He also wrote to the emperor, exhorting him not to impair the integrity of the Catholic faith (*ep.* 3.4). He must adhere to the norm of apostolic doctrine found in the bishop of Rome to whom the Lord has entrusted the care of the whole sheepfold (*ep.* 3.5). The false teachings already cut down by the "evangelical scythe" cannot be brought back to life (*ep.* 3.6). The teaching of Leo and the council have made things perfectly clear and certain so that they cannot be called into question and discussed as if they were doubtful (*ep.* 4.1).

Most of his extant correspondence was written in an unsuccessful attempt to keep emperor and patriarch from succumbing to the temptation to compromise. And in that effort, familiar terms and ideas reappear, for example, the pope is taught by Peter himself (*ep.* 6.2). The council's and Leo's teaching can never be reconsidered or tampered with (*ep.* 5 to Acacius; *ep.* 6.4 to Zeno) because that teaching has been accepted universally and has been approved by heaven (*ep.* 7.5). Bishops, in particular, he warned Acacius, must be vigilant and not allow anything to be done to the contrary through their negligence and laziness (*epp.* 18.1; 20).[25]

Felix II at his accession in 483 was faced with the fact of the *Henoticon*. He condemned it and demanded to no avail that Acacius stop supporting Peter Mongos in Alexandria. In 484, he excommunicated Acacius. Thus began the Acacian schism between Rome and Constantinople that was to last for thirty-five years. The crisis now was more acute. Felix began pleading with the emperor Zeno to accept fully the conciliar and Leonine teaching. Peter spoke up to assert that his faith alone was true. The Lord would not allow it to be overcome (*ep.* 1.3). Any reconsideration of Chalcedon entertained will only appear to reopen the doors to every heresy formerly condemned (*ep.* 1.12).

Felix's office obliges him to take action. Even if Acacius will not listen to him, he should not forget that he, like every bishop, has an obligation to be concerned for the integrity of the Catholic faith, the safeguarding of the traditions of the Fathers and the decisions of the council of Chalcedon (*ep.* 2.1, 3). Like his great predecessor Athanasius, the orthodox Patriarch of Alexandria, John Talaia, was forced to flee his see and take refuge in Rome (*ep.* 3.1). An appeal to the emperor to make his Patriarch behave, did no good, naturally enough since the Patriarch was just doing what the emperor wanted him to do. Felix wrote the emperor: "He tried to hide behind your name" (*ep.* 8.4). Learn from the bishops, the emperor was told; do not try to teach them (*ep.* 8.5).[26]

The opportunity for a speedy resolution of the conflict presented itself at the end of the decade when Acacius died in 489, (Zeno in 491). But there was no such resolution. The new Patriarchs, Fravita very briefly, then Euphemius, 490-496, were orthodox and repudiated Peter Mongos. They explicitly upheld Chalcedon. But the schism continued because they refused to repudiate and condemn their predecessor Acacius. Part of the motivation for this refusal revolved around the question of whether the bishop of Rome by himself, without a council, or at least, without the agreement of the patriarchs, had the authority to depose the Patriarch of Constantinople.

The schism continued on that basis for another twenty-nine years. It has sometimes been called the schism of the diptychs. Rome's position was that as executrix of the council of

Chalcedon, it had rightly excommunicated Acacius. If nothing had been done, Rome could have been regarded as an accomplice of his heresy (*ep.* 17.2). Given that background, it is not surprising that Felix (and even more, Gelasius a little later) had to defend himself against the charge of perverse stubbornness. Felix protested that he was only defending the teaching of the Fathers (*ep.* 14.3).[27]

Gelasius (492-496)

The second great Pope of the fifth century was Gelasius,[28] a Roman, possibly of North African origins. Unlike Leo he was bishop for only a short time, from 492-496. However, like Leo, he did not suddenly appear on the Roman scene with his election. He had been active in the curia for some time and was no doubt very influential, at least from the beginning of the Acacian schism. The first letter traditionally assigned to his corpus probably appeared during the pontificate of Felix but can be assigned with confidence not only to the inspiration of Gelasius but probably to his pen as well. I see in Gelasius the high point of papal claims in Antiquity.

It has been suggested by A.S. McGrade that there is a qualitative change in the teaching on Roman authority from Leo to Gelasius. He terms Leo's views ecumenical and inclusive vs. the papalist, exclusive position of Gelasius. I am not convinced of such a qualitative shift. Rather I see the same basic teaching being expressed in two different styles by two types of men. Gelasius adopts a more arrogant paternalistic tone in dealing with the emperor but Celestine had long before insisted that laymen are to be docile to bishops and leave doctrinal decisions to clerics. Gelasius was not the first to urge that governmental pressure and, if necessary, coercion be used to enforce orthodoxy. I too would see Leo's style as "more cooperative," expressing less of a constant sense of superiority than Gelasius' style. But the theological foundational thinking of both is the same.

Most of the significant correspondence of Gelasius is with eastern figures, especially with the unsympathetic emperor

Anastasius and with the successors of Acacius in Constantinople. His western correspondence carries on the pattern we
have seen earlier. Writing to bishop Honorius of Salona in
Dalmatia, he speaks of his concern for all the churches, a
concern which does not allow him to remain silent. Like Peter,
he has charge of the entire flock of the Lord and the command
to confirm the brethren (*ep.* 4.1). A Roman council of March
495 recorded the following acclamations: "We see the Apostle
Peter in you" (six times), and for the first time in history: "We
see you as the vicar of Christ" (seven times) (*ep.* 30.15).

But the great bulk of Gelasius' writing deals with the eastern
problem, a situation that was becoming more intractable every
year. As recently as the time of Leo, the bishop of Thessalonika
had continued as the faithful vicar for Rome, but the incum-
bent bishop was among those who refused to drop the name
of Acacius from the diptychs (*ep.* 18.4). Some of Gelasius'
most significant letters were sent to the bishops of Dardania,
an area equivalent to the southernmost section of modern
Yugoslavia. He had a hard time convincing them of the justice
of the Roman position (esp. *ep.* 26).

To the orthodox Patriarch Euphemius, who nonetheless
refused to repudiate his predecessor Acacius, Gelasius wrote
that while he appreciated Euphemius' compliments for his
(Gelasius') office, he would much prefer to see some follow-
through in the way of obedient compliance (*ep.* 3.4).[29] Keeping
faith with Acacius is to flirt with the heresy of the Alexandrian
Patriarch with whom Acacius was in communion. Avoid that
contagion and return to the unblemished faith and communion
of the Roman church, kept inviolate by Gelasius (*ep.* 3.12, 14).
One novel angle in this letter is that the frequently praised
faith of the Roman people is here said to be so pure and
praiseworthy because Gelasius keeps it so (*ep.* 3.15). This is
said in the context of urging that the role of the bishop is not
to accept what his people believe but to command or at least
to direct it.

The eastern objections against Roman procedure and
actions are without merit. Looking back on a century and a
half, Gelasius noted that, as in the case of Athanasius and
John Chrysostom, Rome had frequently rejected condem-

nations pronounced by eastern councils, sometimes without the benefit of a western council (*epp.* 1.1; 26.4). Since the case of Acacius was related to the status of the bishop of Alexandria, and since there had always been a special relationship between the first and second sees, this was one more reason why Rome should have been involved from the beginning (*ep.* 1.9).

Rome has the *cura* of the universal Church (*ep.* 1.26). The authority of the apostolic see has extended to the whole Church in every century. This is confirmed by the series of canons of the Fathers (an expression commonly used by Gelasius) and multiple traditions. Is anyone prepared to reject the canons of Nicaea (*ep.* 12.9)?[30] This brings up again the Roman habit of attaching the appeal canons of Sardica to the canons of Nicaea. Early in the fifth century, the Africans had called the attention of Romans to the error but this corrective apparently had effected no change in the Roman practice. There was also circulating an interpolated western version of the sixth canon of Nicaea which stated flatly that the Roman church had always had the primacy. This had been presented at Chalcedon by the Roman representatives but had been rejected as inauthentic. But this rebuff had made no dent in Roman self-assurance.

In the same spirit, with supreme self-confidence, Gelasius wrote to Faustus, his representative in Constantinople:

> They oppose us with the canons but they do not know what they are talking about. . . . The canons themselves willed the appeals of the whole Church to be referred to the examination of this see. From it, they also decreed that no appeal whatever ought to be made, and thereby that it should judge the whole Church and come under the judgment of none. They determined that its sentence should not be annulled but ordered its decrees to be complied with.
>
> By what tradition of the ancestors do they call the apostolic see to judgment? Let them see therefore if they have other canons with which they may pursue their fooleries. . . . What religious and excellent men? They try to shatter the power which certainly has been granted to the

> apostolic see under the canons and strive to usurp to themselves what is contrary to the canons. . . .
>
> We are in no fear lest the apostolic judgment be reversed, something which both the voice of Christ and the traditions of the Fathers, as also the authority of the canons support, in such wise that rather it may always judge the whole Church (*ep.* 10.5-6).

The gates of Hell cannot prevail against the confession of Peter the Apostle (*ep.* 10.9).

But it is probably his letter 26 of February 495, written to the wavering bishops of the province of Dardania, caught between the two forces of Rome and Constantinople, that contains his fullest exposition both of his view of the entire controversy and of the Roman position and authority.

> The see of blessed Peter the Apostle has the right to unbind what has been bound by sentences of any pontiffs whatsoever, in that it has the right of judging the whole Church. Neither is it lawful for anyone to judge its judgment, seeing that the canons have willed that it may be appealed to from any part of the world, but that no one may be allowed to appeal from it (*ep.* 26.5).[31]

In the matter of councils, the second council of Ephesus (449) was rejected by Rome, overruling the second see, Alexandria, and its bishop, Dioscuros. "As what the first see did not approve could not stand, so what it decided must be done, the whole Church accepted" (*ep.* 26.5). Here and in his treatise on the Anathema, he listed the attributes of the "good" council, the *synodus bene gesta.* Such a council is in accordance with Scripture, the Tradition of the Fathers, the ecclesiastical rules for the Catholic faith and communion, received by the whole Church, and, last but not least, indeed one might say more appropriately, most of all, approved by the apostolic see (*ep.* 26.6).

Whether these conditions have been met in a given case may be a matter of debate. Is Ephesus 449 or Chalcedon 451 more in accord with Scripture and Tradition? It is the apostolic see that decides ultimately. All the criteria listed by Gelasius are open to debate save the last. Papal approval or lack of it are matters of historical record and thus in the long run can easily become the only criterion of practical relevance. It has frequently been said that the violence and coercion which accompanied a council like that of 449 made it even more obviously unacceptable and void. Was the very acceptable council of 431 much better? On the other hand, a disservice was done to the Church when the solid results of councils like Nicaea and Chalcedon are de facto brought into doubt and rendered uncertain by renewing debate over the issues they were supposed to have settled (*Idem*).

Some of his harsher and more sarcastic remarks are also found in this letter 26. When faced with the claim that Constantinople should have a more important place in the Church because it is the imperial city, Gelasius tells us that he laughed. Emperors had also lived in Ravenna, Sirmium, and Trier among other cities; of what importance are they now (*ep.* 26.10)? By canonical tradition, Constantinople should not even be numbered among the metropolitan sees, let alone be considered the second see. As far as Gelasius was concerned, Constantinople was still just a suffragan see of the metropolitan of Heraclea (*ep.* 26.4, 5, 10)![32] In sum, he wrote to the bishops of Dardania, the Holy See has done nothing wrong whatsoever (*ep.* 26.16). On the contrary, by holding its council in Italy against Acacius, it acted in accordance with Chalcedon, doing what Rome has always done, working for an untainted faith and communion (*ep.* 26.14). In a letter written shortly thereafter to the eastern bishops, Gelasius more modestly complained that they did not have a case against Rome because they knew very well that in such instances Rome was always to be consulted but it had not been (*ep.* 27.9-10).

The traditionalist strain in Gelasius is at least as strong, if not stronger than in his predecessors. He frequently referred not just to Tradition but to the traditions of the Fathers and the rules as well as to the canons which must be adhered to. In the fear of a revival of Pelagianism, he wrote to Honorius of Salona that this was a heresy condemned long ago by our ancestors (*epp.* 4-5). As he sometimes notes, these ancestors were superior to us in virtue and intelligence (*ep.* 4.2). To attempt to reconsider past decisions now only tends to weaken the old condemnations. Writing about a variety of disciplinary questions, he reminded the bishops of Picenum to stand by tradition with the separation of the sexes in church (*ep.* 6.9). Gelasius always followed the pathways of the ancient faith and communion, he told abbot Natalis (*ep.* 8.1). In a later letter (494) to the bishops of the Abruzzi and Sicily, he admonished them to abolish abuses and novelities and to return to the canons of the Fathers earlier abandoned (*ep.* 14.1). This can easily be done by conforming in all ways to the customs of the see of Peter, to which the Lord had entrusted the leadership (principatus) of the entire Church (*ep.* 14.9).[33]

The very same arguments were used against eastern objections and sceptics. It was simply presumed without proof that the Roman position was the view of the ancients. Since one must not go against the ancients, then all must conform to the Roman position. There must be no innovations; the ancients were better than we are. If only all would obey the rules, there would be no problems in the Church (*ep.* 1.19). To the emperor Anastasius, he explained that the matter was uncomplicated. This is the way that God had established things and nothing was to be changed (*ep.* 12.3). To the bishops of Dardania, he urged the necessity of making a choice: if they were in communion with the eastern heretics, they could not also be in communion with Rome (*ep.* 18.2). They must choose the right way and make efforts to get others to do the same (*ep.* 18.3, 6). In the later and more severe letter 26, he told the same bishops that, in opposing Acacius, the apostolic see had simply done what it had to do. Acacius knew it but ignored Roman warnings (*ep.* 26.3, 4). Why keep arguing about it? The case is as clear as it can be. Old heresies are dead and cannot be revived though, just talking about them may give people the impression that they are still living options and that certitudes are no longer as certain as they once seemed (*ep.* 26.1). All are to believe with one heart and confess with one mouth what we have received from our forebears and pass that and that alone on to posterity (*Tract.* III.16). Do you have any hesitations about what this is? Ask Rome: "In accordance with the Scriptures, the tradition of the Fathers, and the canons and rules of the Church, what the apostolic see has appointed to be done and has confirmed when done, is admitted by the whole Church for common faith and apostolic truth (*Treatise on the Anathema 1*).

In his correspondence with the East on the question of Acacius, Gelasius openly confronted the charge that he was being arrogant and stubborn. He was variously said to be: "harsh, pitiless, too hard and difficult" (*ep.* 3.16).[34] His answer was that humility was being what you are, not denying it, and that Rome was supreme. Further, he noted that medicine may be very bitter but you will die if you don't take it. Nor was he above making insulting remarks in return as when he noted that heresies abounded among the Greeks (*ep.* 7.2). Or, as he noted later, when asked why he did not try to hold a council with easterners to try to resolve the Acacius case, he asked simply with whom he might be able to hold such a council? The heretics controlled the East and had driven out the orthodox prelates (*ep.* 26.9).

In his general defense he maintained that the dignity of the apostolic see is not lessened by being stubborn in the condemnation of heretics. On the contrary, it is fulfilling its principal role in defending the Catholic faith and communion (*ep.* 1.33, 41). Further, Gelasius felt an obligation to stand by and support those bishops in the East who had supported him to their cost (*ep.* 1.39). His job was to condemn heretics; if he did not, he would be presumed either to approve them, or at least, to tolerate them (*ep.* 1.21). What would be the result of this? The apostolic see itself would become tainted (something that is impossible). Gelasius would be guilty of giving in to Acacius. And finally, if that happened, who would be left to offer a remedy? (And this is something God would not allow to come about.) Not Rome, for it too would now be in need of a remedy (*ep.* 1.27, 34). Is Gelasius embarrassed by being alone in this extreme stand? Not at all. The Apostles had the truth at the beginning but were few in number too (*ep.* 1.42). Rome must keep itself free from all pollution (*ep.* 3.1). Later, he repeated the same arguments to the emperor Anastasius. Rome is not being arrogant but offers a bitter but necessary remedy to the sick (*ep.* 12.12). The Catholic faith is that one which is clean of all heresy, a communion that is pure and immaculate. Were it to disappear, nothing would be left but miserable confusion. Thus the apostolic see fears heresy very much and keeps itself pure lest there be no place left from which correction could come forth (*ep.* 12.5, 6).

Gelasius accepted no excuses. Acacius was forced by the emperor to take the stand that he did? Then why not martyrdom (*ep.* 1.25)?[35] The people of Alexandria wanted Peter Mongos as their bishop? You cannot give in to the people. As Celestine had put it, the people are to be taught, not followed (*ep.* 1.13). And he added in *ep.* 3.15, you will have to give an account to God for their faith. They will not have to give an account for you!

As a Roman, Gelasius protested to Anastasius, he loved and honored the emperor (even though Rome was at the time under the rule of the Ostrogothic king of Italy). As a Christian, Gelasius wanted the emperor's zeal for the faith to be according to the correct knowledge of the faith. Further as "vicar of the Apostolic see," he had a duty to instruct the emperor (*ep.* 12.1) and to see to the maintenance of orthodoxy. In Church matters especially in questions of doctrine, emperors were subject to bishops (*ep.* 1.10).[36] He is a son, not a ruler, of the Church (*Idem*). Prophetic of the centuries to come in the West, Pope Gelasius outlined his view of power in the world in this famous passage from letter 12:

> I beg your Piety not to judge duty to divine truth as arrogance. I hope that it will not have to be said of a Roman emperor that he resented the truth being brought home to him. There are indeed, most august emperor, two powers by which this world is chiefly ruled: the sacred authority of the Popes and the royal power. Of these, the priestly power is much more important, because it has to render an account for the kings of men themselves at the divine tribunal. For you know, our very clement son, that although you have the chief place in dignity over the human race, yet you must submit yourself faithfully to those who have charge of divine

things and look to them for the means of your salvation. You know that it behooves you in matters concerning the reception and reverent administration of the sacraments, to be obedient to the ecclesiastical authority rather than to control it.... So just as there is great danger for Popes in not saying what is necessary in matters of the divine honor, so there is no small peril for those who are obstinate in resistance ... at the time when they ought to be obedient. And if the hearts of the Faithful ought to be submitted to all priests in general, who administer holy things in a right manner, how much more ought assent to be given to him who presides over that see which the supreme Godhead itself desired to be pre-eminent over all priests and which the pious judgment of the whole Church has honored ever since (*ep.* 12.2)?[37]

The Acacian schism was to last until the coming of Justinian who at first renewed Byzantine relations with Rome in an initial show of respect but eventually was to bring down the Roman see to its point of humiliation in the mid-sixth century. Had Gelasius' hard line effected the desired result? No. But the very modest "ecumenical" conciliatory gestures of his successor, Pope Anastasius II, brought about the extraordinary condemnatory phrase found in the *Liber pontificalis,* the papacy's own version of its history, that because of his "soft-line", "God struck him dead" (*Liber pontificalis* 52).

VII

An Irresistible Rise?
A Bump in the Road of
Roman Progress in the Sixth Century

During the remainder of the reign of the eastern emperor Anastasius, the status quo of schism and ill feelings was maintained. But with his death in July of 518, there acceded to the throne in Constantinople a soldier of Illyrian peasant origin, Justin I (518-527). Despite a lack of formal education, he had risen to a high post in the military, though it is unlikely that he was illiterate as Procopius asserted in his *Anecdota* or Secret History. It may be argued whether Justin was more of a westerner in his background and outlook than many of his immediate predecessors. In any event, it was clear from the outset that the supporters of Chalcedon now had a friend on the throne. A high priority for Justin and his nephew Justinian was the ending of the Acacian schism. Thus on September 7 of the same year, Justin, Justinian, and the Patriarch John II all wrote to Pope Hormisdas (514-23) with this great purpose in mind.

The next year the papal delegates arrived in Constantinople with an instrument designed to restore unity at once but strictly on Roman terms. It was clear that the civil power wanted peace and was determined to get it. What was uncertain was how far they were ready to go to force the eastern ecclesiastical authorities to submit to what some no doubt considered humiliating, if not unacceptable, terms. With some reluctance, the Patriarch John brought himself to sign although he tried to soften the blow somewhat by adding his own unusual formula: "I hold the most holy churches of God, that is, yours of Elder Rome and this of New Rome are one; I define the see of the Apostle Peter and this of the imperial city to be one see." Elsewhere much more open opposition was in evidence. Justin did what he could to pressure bishops into acceptance, and Rome accepted the imperfect results as satisfactory.

The formula of reunion put forward by Pope Hormisdas[1] is noteworthy for a phrase that is significant not just in the history of the Roman primacy, but more specifically for the pre-history of papal infallibility. "The first condition of salvation is to keep the norm of the true faith and in no way to deviate from the established doctrine of the Fathers. For it is impossible that the words of Our Lord Jesus Christ who said, "thou are Peter and upon this rock I will build my Church" (Matthew 16:18), should not be verified. And their truth has been proven by the course of history, for in the apostolic see the Catholic religion has always been kept unsullied "(. . . *quia in Sede apostolica immaculata est semper catholica servata religio*). He went on to rub it in by specifying among the first heretics to be anathematized Nestorius, a bishop of Constantinople.

In 527, Justin's nephew, Justinian, succeeded to the throne, beginning one of the longest and most eventful reigns of early Byzantine history.[2] Of fateful importance for Rome was Justinian's ambition to liberate the West from barbarian domination and to reconstitute the earlier Roman empire in its glory. While the first steps were accomplished with ease against the Vandals in North Africa in 533, the reconquest of Italy turned into a disaster and a horror, bringing famine, pestilence, and the long agony of competing armies fighting back and forth over the length of the peninsula. Ironically for Rome, it removed the relatively benign rule of the Arian Ostrogothic kings which had served as a buffer and filter against imperial authority in far-off Constantinople. Now the imperial will and displeasure made themselves felt directly in the streets and churches of Old Rome. The high point of Hormisdas' triumphal formula of reunion was to give way to the sad spectacle of Pope Vigilius' captivity and humiliation in Constantinople. His doctrinal vacillation brought papal prestige in the West to its lowest point in ancient times.

Vigilius (537-555)

From the time of Pope Damasus (366-384), the documentary evidence for Roman authority is abundant. The tone of papal correspondence is one of command, of supreme authority and undisputed primacy, unclouded by hesitation or shadow of self-doubt. No wonder, for the assertion is often repeated, that it is not Damasus or Siricius who commands; it is still Peter present somehow but really in each successive bishop of Rome. There were some further advances, of course, as when Zosimus and Boniface (417-422) first clearly stated that Roman decisions were open neither to appeal nor to reconsideration. Whether it was the gentlemanly and amiable Leo or the imperious and sarcastic Gelasius, the position of world leadership is presumed by the Roman *stylus curiae*. This air of untroubled supremacy is still found in the earlier letters of Pope Vigilius.[3] He wrote, for example, to bishop Profuturus of Braga: the Roman church is the foundation and form of all the churches (*ep.* 1.7. A.D. 538). None of the faithful is unaware that all the churches are to be referred to it. In 545, the year of his forced departure from Rome, he wrote to bishop Auxanius of Arles that stability came from the rock of Peter in Rome. All disputes which cannot be settled in Gaul are to be referred to Rome for decision (*ep.* 7).

The seemingly uncontested and irresistible rise met a serious obstacle and detour in the affair of the Three Chapters of the mid-sixth century. The emperor Justinian (527-565) had earlier been very respectful of the Roman see. But it was his later efforts to try to reunite the non-Chalcedonian dissidents that would bring trouble. He too succumbed to the temptation which had seduced earlier emperors in the fifth century. Even here, Popes John II (533-535) and Agapitus (535-536) both surprisingly approved his favored Theopaschite formula, even though Pope Hormisdas had disapproved of it. Justinian in return wrote to Agapitus in March 536, echoing the famous claim of the formula of Hormisdas that *in sede apostolica inviolabiliter semper catholica custoditur religio (Collectio Avellana* 89).

Unfortunately the harmony was not to last. Justinian, probably persuaded by Theodore Askidas whom he had made archbishop of Caesarea in Cappadocia, decided to take a further step he hoped would please the Monophysites. This, of course, was the beginning of the controversy that came to be known as "The Three Chapters." Three men and some of their writings were at issue: Theodore of Mopsuestia (+ 428), teacher of Nestorius, and his writings; the writings of Theodoret of Cyrrhus (+ c. 466) against Cyril of Alexandria; and the letter of Ibas of Edessa (+ 457) to the Persian bishop Maris. Such a measure against three viewed loosely at least as Nestorians, it was hoped, would appease the dissidents sufficiently to lead to some sort of rapprochement. And so they were condemned for the first time by Justinian in 543-44.

Few had any sympathy for the unfortunate and misunderstood Theodore. But the cases of the other two were more debatable. Theodoret, for years the principal theologian of the school of Antioch and probable author of the formula of reunion between Antioch and Alexandria adopted in 433, had surely said many harsh things against the dissidents' hero, Cyril of Alexandria. Deposed by the robber council of 449, he was reinstated by Pope Leo and, after publicly anathematizing Nestorius, approved as well by a more sceptical council of Chalcedon in 451. Herein lay the problem: How to condemn Theodore who had died in the peace of the Church shortly before the Nestorius controversy broke out? How to condemn someone like Theodoret who, whatever the earlier hesitations, had been accepted by Leo and Chalcedon? As for Ibas of Edessa, his letter had been full of criticism of Cyril, accusing him of Apollinarianism. If the council had otherwise found the man acceptable, had it also approved the letter?

The West reacted strongly to any such suggestions which were seen in general as an attack on Leo and the council of Chalcedon, Leo's council. Vigilius was forcibly taken from Rome in 545, arriving in Constantinople on January 25, 547.

His story at Constantinople is a long and sad one, filled with vacillation, hesitations, and equivocation. While he refused to attend Justinian's council in the imperial city in 553, he ultimately capitulated and approved the council's decrees the next year. He died en route back to Italy in 555, leaving his successors to face the firestorm. As a foretaste of things to come, the African bishops, themselves only recently liberated by Justinian's forces from the harsh, century-long Vandal occupation, were among the leading critics of Vigilius and had already in 550 withdrawn from communion with him.

Here we are primarily interested in the positions taken by Vigilius' successors in defending themselves against the generalized western perception that Vigilius' temporizing and ultimate coming down on the side of Justinian's council were a betrayal of what the Papacy had stood for for a century—Leo and Chalcedon. Worse still, it seemed to signal a failure in the principal claim of Rome to defend the apostolic teaching—its role of *vigilantia*.

Vigilius' immediate successor, Pelagius I (556-561), was in the worst position, not just because he was the immediate heir to western anger and frustration, but also because, as Vigilius' deacon, he had authored a treatise whose point was that the Three Chapters could *not* be lawfully condemned.[4] His rapid turnabout was demanded no doubt by the emperor as the price of imperial approval of him as Vigilius' successor. But when he returned to Rome, he faced a cold reception. Not even the customary minimum of three bishops could be found to ordain him bishop of Rome. Most of his episcopate was taken up with self-defense.

Faced with schismatic movements at worst and suspicions at best, Pelagius moved to strengthen his position but only with indifferent success. And the Papacy found itself in an unaccustomed posture of continual self-justification and even occasional self-deprecation. Pelagius made repeated assertions of his own orthodoxy, of his acceptance of the first four councils. There is rarely a mention of the fifth. He even wrote an open letter "to the People of God" in 557 (*ep.* 11), giving his confession of faith for examination by all the world. The one thing that is not found is a detailed explanation of the issues, namely, of how Vigilius could have ultimately agreed with his initial position expressed in the *In Defensione trium Capitulorum* to his acceptance of the council. Here, in *ep.* 11 and elsewhere, his defense is always framed in the most general terms. Only in passing at the end of *ep.* 11 does he mention his general approval of Theodoret of Cyrrhus and Ibas of Edessa (*ep.* 11.10).[5]

Is this not another example of a phenomenon that happens not infrequently in church history? One part affirms two or more statements and claims that there is no incompatibility between or among them. But the other party protests precisely because it cannot see or understand these simultaneous affirmations inasmuch as it perceives an incompatibility between or among them. The first party is unwilling or unable to explain how the statements are not incompatible.

Pelagius first tried to stanch the flow of criticism and scepticism by blaming slanderous rumors and false reports. He advised the Frankish king Childebert and the Gallic bishops not to listen to stories of men who delighted in scandals (*ep.* 3.1). From beginning to end of his episcopate, one common rumor that circulated widely was that Pelagius had written a letter from Constantinople, protesting that the council had corrupted the Catholic faith. Anonymous enemies spread such tales, he protested to Childebert (*ep.* 3.4-5). But at the end of his pontificate, he was still protesting. In letter 80, he specified that while he had written no such letter, he did write a treatise against the condemnation of the Three Chapters.

These rumors, exaggerations, and false stories have led people into serious errors (*ep.* 38). He urged bishop Sapaudus of Arles and the Gallic bishops to forsake these false teachings and return to unity (*ep.* 19.22, 24). They should know better, but many others err out of simple ignorance (*ep.* 11.2). In addition to his real or alleged writings directly concerning events in Constantinople, Sapaudus and his Gallic colleagues also brought up an earlier letter which Pelagius had written as a deacon to Ferrandus of Carthage seeking the latter's theological advice on the matter at hand (*ep.* 19.1). (Ferrandus, one of the leading western theologians of the day, had advised strongly against condemning the Three Chapters.)

Earlier in his pontificate, Pelagius, while generally on the defensive, could also occasionally express indignation at the lack of respect shown the apostolic see by certain bishops. The bishops of Tuscia Annonaria to whom he wrote his *ep.* 10 in April of 557 were omitting his name from the eucharistic celebration. They were forgetting the authority of the apostolic see and threatening to lead public opinion, ignorant as it always is of theological issues, into a similar lack of respect. Elsewhere he argued that the bishops in Gaul had no right to dissent when other bishops found no problems with the Roman position. He recalled that the African church was now in complete submission, omitting to mention that this calm had been achieved only by imperial coercion (*ep.* 19.17).[6]

Not surprisingly in the correspondence of a Roman bishop, the need for unity in the Church is given a prominent place in the campaign against dissenters. What is unusual here is that the appeal puts much less emphasis on the importance of being in communion with Rome as the center of the Church. Apostolic sees in the plural occurs much more than reference to Rome alone as *the* apostolic see. Cut off from the apostolic churches, the dissident communities dry up like branches, severed from the tree (*ep.* 24.2-3). Cut off from the apostolic root, they do not belong to the one Dove (*ep.* 24.17). They have ceased to be part of the Body of Christ (*ep.* 24.12). Since the Church cannot be divided, schismatics cease to be part of the Church when they leave it (*ep.* 35.13).

With a certain exasperation, he explained to Victor and Pancratius, that since schismatics have forsaken the unity of the Church, one cannot be in communion with them (*ep.* 35.1-2). Needless to say, Pelagius was not amused by the suggestion that it might be the Romans themselves who were the schismatics in this instance (*ep.* 35.11). The gates of Hell cannot prevail against the Church, that Church in which are found *all* the apostolic sees (*ep.* 39). Those who are schismatics sever themselves from these apostolic sees and cannot be called a communion (*ep.* 59.2). Their own local councils do not have precedence over a universal council. If they have difficulties accepting such a general council, they should go to the apostolic sees with their problems (*ep.* 59.8-9).[7]

He frequently invited sceptics and doubters to come to Rome. He expressed the intention of showing much charity to these dissenters (*ep.* 37). But, in fact, charity was not his sole policy. Even as he wrote in more kindly terms to those who had problems with Roman policy, he was also writing to the civil authorities, urging them to use force to coerce the dissidents. In the case of the problems presented by Sapaudus of Arles and the other Gallic bishops, he urged king Childebert to take action lest both the royal and papal authority be lessened, since threats to Church authority should also be regarded as threats to the royal authority (*ep.* 6.3). Therefore, it is in the king's interest to see to it that bishops Sapaudus of Arles be put in his place (*epp.* 8; 7, 17-18).

Perhaps Pelagius' patience was running out as he became frustrated by the lack of results from his more irenic efforts, but his calls for coercive measures became more frequent in his final two years. If troublemakers are unpunished, they only grow bolder (*ep.* 53). He urged the patrician John to go in and clean out the schismatic center of Aquileia. Sometimes he added the request that the schismatic leaders be sent to him in Rome (*ep.* 60.3; 65; 69). The villain, after all, was only a pseudo-bishop. Officials using force against such people will be rewarded by God for doing a good work (*ep.* 69).

Response from the civil authorities to such appeals was often less than enthusiastic. This may have been more for political than humanitarian reasons, to be sure. Pelagius felt obliged to write an apology for the use of coercion in matters of religion. It is no sin to use force against dissidents, he argued. Secular power can be used against those who split the Church and disturb the peace (*ep.* 65). If secular leaders were a bit timid in this matter, Pelagius plied them with arguments from the Fathers, specifying that in the case of schismatics, exile was a possible penalty as well as confiscation of property and even *dura custodia* (*ep.* 60.3).[8]

Such use of force, he wrote to the patrician Valerian, did not constitute a persecution, since to repress someone who does evil is an action taken out of love for that person. If people were not forced to do good and abstain from evil, all human laws would be rendered meaningless (*ep.* 52.5-6). In these letters of Pelagius, there are many citations from Augustine, many of which cannot be verified. Yet in this matter he does make use of Augustine's rationale for the use of coercion in matters of religion. The Church takes such coercive action, or, better, urges the civil power to do so, out of love for the sinner (*ep.* 52.13). By such measures, pride is cast down and humility taught, albeit the hard way (*ep.* 67). He sometimes gave detailed instructions on how to proceed. To Agnellus of Ravenna, he suggested that an ultimatum of ten days be given to the dissidents (*ep.* 74). He had a particular grudge against a certain Paulinus (of Fossombrone?) and urged the civil authority, John the *magister militum* (*ep.* 71) and Basil the *defensor* (*ep.* 70) to pursue him. (This harder line is found especially in the later letters.)

But the most startling aspect of this pontificate lay in Pelagius' attempt to confront the sceptics with uncharacteristic openness. The contrast to the by now traditional Roman tone of complete self-assurance, of the absolute guarantee of continuity of teaching and tradition, of the unquestionability of Roman decisions and teaching is striking. Pelagius felt it necessary continually to assert his orthodoxy, his support for the four councils, (*ep.* 7.2-3 to Childebert; *ep.* 10.4 to the bishops of Tuscia Annonaria), of Leo the Great (*ep.* 11.3, 6). He had changed nothing, deviated from the Fathers in nothing but had kept all things inviolate (*ep.* 10.4).

If there was anyone who did not accept his word on this or who continued to have doubts, he should come to Rome in person or send a representative to interrogate the pope (*ep.* 10.4). Like Saint Peter, Pelagius always stood ready to give a reason for the faith that was in him (I Peter 3:15; cf. *epp.* 7.16; 11.10; 19.25). Even late in his pontificate he said that if the schismatics did not accept his word, let them send two or three *docti viri* to examine him (*ep.* 59.6-7).[9]

The tactic that was most dangerous from the point of view of Roman tradition was his habit of asking from time to time: What is wrong with changing? He cited Cyprian (*ep.* 71.3) who remarked that as Peter was corrected by Paul (Galatians 2:11), so it was fitting to be open to better ideas suggested by brothers and colleagues (*ep.* 19.3 of Pelagius). In his old age,

Augustine wrote his *Retractationes* to show how his mind had changed on various matters (*ep.* 19.17).[10] Such thoughts were dangerous for the Roman tradition, of course, because previous popes had emphasized that their decisions were not open to reconsideration or appeal.

As the years went on in the sixth century, slowly the sceptics and dissidents returned to the Roman fold and the schism came to center in Istria and the see of Aquileia in particular. Pelagius I had the most troubled pontificate. His general assertions of orthodoxy failed to convince the recalcitrant, and he never engaged in a detailed justification of his support for the council and the condemnation of the Three Chapters. He did not address the question most in need of a convincing answer. One may wonder whether such an effort would have helped since the unfortunate Vigilius in his time at Constantinople had worked out tortured, detailed analyses of the issues, but in so doing had come to contradictory conclusions, the final decision depending much more on imperial pressure than on historical or theological arguments.

Pelagius II (579-590)

The schism was progressively confined to northeastern Italy. Pelagius II carried on a dialogue with the bishops of Istria on the same issue in the hope of bringing about a reunion. His first letter was similar to the plea of Pelagius I. Stressing that the faith of Peter could not be shaken (Luke 22:31-2), he proceeded on the presupposition that the papal position should *a priori* be considered the correct one (*ep.* 1.5-6). Like his predecessor, he urged the northern bishops to send delegates to discuss his faith with him. Citing 1 Peter 3:15, he emphasized his willingness to give satisfaction (*ep.* 1.15-16) about *fidei nostrae integritate* (*ep.* 1.7). He affirmed his unqualified acceptance of the first four councils; that he had kept inviolate the apostolic tradition and that of his predecessors, and that he would defend the same to the shedding of his blood (*ep.* 1.8). In particular, he venerated, defended, and supported Leo's doctrine and the council of Chalcedon (*ep.* 1.13). Doubters should be satisfied with this and avoid further questions which would be useless in any case (Scriptural references to Colossians 2.8 and II Timothy 2:23-24).

This initial plea brought not a peace-making delegation from the North but a letter reiterating their condemnation of the Roman position (*ep.* 2.1-2). Pelagius' reply stressed the evil of schism and the necessity of being in communion with the apostolic sees (*ep.* 2.20). Paul had exhorted to charity, but the dissidents were exhibiting only pride and stubbornness (*ep.* 2.17-18). One new element here is that Pelagius II clearly states his view that the council of Chalcedon had made irrevocable decisions only on the definition of faith. Matters concerning *privatae causae,* discussions which came after the definition of faith not only were not irreversible decisions but were explicitly, he says, commended for reconsideration by future judges (*ep.* 2.9, 13-14). It may be, of course, that what Pelagius was referring to concerned primarily canon 28.[11]

Since these first two letters had accomplished nothing, the future Pope Gregory I, having returned from Constantinople where he had served as papal representative, was set to work to write a detailed reply to the now long-standing criticisms. This was to become Pelagius' third letter to the bishops of Istria, the only time the popes turned to a step-by-step discussion of what had been done by Vigilius and Justinian's council of Constantinople.

He argued that while the faith of the council of Chalcedon had not been and must not be shaken (*ep.* 3.13), learned men realized that Pope Leo had not approved of everything done in the council and had been careful to make distinctions where necessary (*ep.* 3.38). Vigilius and the western bishops originally opposed the condemnation of the Three Chapters because they did not understand Greek and the eastern point of view. Once they went to Constantinople and began to understand, they changed their position and agreed to the condemnation (*ep.* 3.53).

If the northern dissidents would only pay attention, they, too, would see the virtue of switching rather than fighting. Paul's preaching of Christianity was all the more impressive and to be taken seriously because of his earlier opposition and violent resistance to change (*ep.* 3.57). Similarly, given the stubborn initial resistance of Vigilius and Pelagius I, the reasons for their change of view must be considered all the more overwhelming (*ep.* 3.58).

Peter changed as well (Galatians 2:11-12). Even God changes His words, though never his strategy (*consilium*) (*ep.* 3.61). Thus a change of words is not important, when new insight is gained, while the basic intention is maintained unchanged (*ep.* 3.60). The dissidents do not recognize this important distinction and in effect keep repeating: "I won't listen to you now because you used to say something different" (*ep.* 3.59).[12]

The dissidents further objected to the condemnation of a dead man, especially one who had died in the peace of the Church such as Theodore of Mopsuestia. Making use of Vigilius' work, including the *Constitutum* of 553, which was rejected by Justinian's council as insufficient, Pelagius II found many of Theodore's words eminently damnable (*ep.* 3.45, 67f.). Invoking Augustine's *ep.* 185.4, Pelagius argued that there was nothing wrong with condemning a dead heretic (*ep.* 3.63). Indeed, given that Theodore wrote so much, he deserved greater torments (*ep.* 3.84).

Theodoret was treated very briefly in *ep.* 3.96 (as was the case also in Vigilius). The letter of Ibas was treated at greater length in Vigilius' second *Judicatum* of February 554. In Pelagius' argumentation, the contents of the letter attacking Cyril were deemed completely unacceptable and could not possibly have been approved by the council. Indeed, if one believed such a contradiction possible, he argued, then you would be the one weakening the *firmitas* of the council's dogmatic definitions (*ep.* 3.102, 104). Indeed, approval of the letter's contents would undermine the council of Ephesus of 431 as well. After claiming that all of Chalcedon's work came in the first six sessions anyway, Pelagius sought to demonstrate that Leo in his letter to Maximus of Antioch (*ep.* 119.5) specifically allowed for the reconsideration of other issues concerning persons (*ep.* 3.115-119). All these factors make it difficult to understand why some people are so upset about the condemnation of the letter (*ep.* 3.122).

There is a brief return to the case of Theodoret. Only his

writings criticizing Cyril are condemned. It is claimed that he himself repudiated them (by anathematizing Nestorius at the council). If Theodoret did so, what is wrong with our condemning them? People make mistakes but correct them, just as Jerome had first praised Origen before seeing the light (*ep.* 3.140, 147). The letter ends with a reiteration of Pelagius' faith and acceptance of the first four councils.[13]

Gregory the Great (590-604)

Following the discouraging lack of results from the extended explanation given in this letter, government action was not long in coming. The arrest of Severus, bishop of Aquileia, and others followed. Their "conversion," however, was short-lived (*ep.* I.16). So Gregory inherited the schism when he became pope. In a sense, he gave up arguing; all that he had to say he had said in Pelagius' third letter. He had ceased to believe in the dissidents' good faith and saw the schism only as an excuse. "They are enveloped so far in the blindness of their ignorance for no other reasons but to escape from ecclesiastical discipline and have license to live perversely as they please, since they understand neither what they defend nor what they follow" (*ep.* VIII.4 of September, 597).

Gregory did not totally abandon the old tactics, however. He had not given up assuring doubters of the orthodoxy of the Roman bishop. In a well-known declaration, he assured one correspondent that he regarded the first four councils as the four Gospels (*ep.* III.10). Nothing had been done in the time of Justinian to violate the faith (*epp.* II.43; III.10). When a Roman cleric, Constantius, became bishop of Milan in 593, Gregory advised him to assure his people that he, Gregory, completely accepted Chalcedon. In the classic formula, he dared add nothing to the definition nor to subtract anything from it (*ep.* IV.3). One of the Milanese doubters was Queen Theodelinda of the Lombards who had withdrawn from communion with Constantius and whom Gregory sought to reassure directly. She should have no concern about the firmness of the Church of Peter the Apostle (*ep.* IV.33; July 594). But a few years later, she apparently had not been sufficiently convinced because he had to assure her once again against slanderous rumors (*ep.* XIV.12; December 603).[14]

Sceptics were still being invited to come and see for themselves. If political difficulties prevented them from coming to Rome, they might find sufficient reassurance in Ravenna (*ep.* II.25). There had been enough pressure exerted in the past that dissenters now demanded guarantees that they would not be coerced if they should come to discuss reunion (*ep.* IV.41 to Boniface; *ep.* V.56 to the Istrian bishops Peter and Providentius). Such guarantees were even offered to Severus of Aquileia who only recently had been arrested and brought to Ravenna where he had been forced into an (illusory) unity (*ep.* I.16).

During Gregory's pontificate, there was a steady trickle of returnees such as Felix, a deacon (*ep.* IV.14) and John, a *religiosus* (*ep.* VI.38; A.D. 596). Civil officials were urged to offer protection to those who wished to return (*ep.* XIII.34). Some clerics from the diocese of Como wanted to know if they could be assured of the return of some property if they came back into unity (*ep.* IX.187). Gregory was eager to assure them of his compliance. Despite many frustrations, Gregory kept trying and urged others not to abandon their efforts for unity in weariness (*ep.* II.38). In moments of anger, Gregory also could urge that force be used "pour encourager les autres." Invoking Augustine's axiom used against the Donatists, *Causa, non poena, facit martyrem,* he denied that coercion used against the dissidents was persecution. Their cause is unjust (*ep.* II.43). Officials must exert extra efforts for unity (*ep.* IX.154; A.D. 599).

Most of all, Gregory was increasingly convinced that sheer perverse stubbornness was holding up the reunion. The third letter of Pelagius had explained everything in great detail surely sufficient to convince anyone of good will. The real reason for such stubborn refusal of unity now was sheer pride (*tumor*) and recalcitrance (*ep.* II.43). Perverse men were using this quarrel as an occasion for disturbing the discipline of the Church. Complaints about faith were merely an excuse (*ep.* IX.148). Indeed, he claimed to have received reports about the *pravitas* of the dissident bishops in Istria (*ep.* IX.202; A.D. 599).[15]

Yet despite his best efforts, the frustrations kept coming.

Constantius of Milan had many difficulties with his episcopal neighbors on this issue (*ep.* IV.2). The Bishop of Brixen and his flock demanded from Constantius an oath in writing that he supported the Three Chapters (*ep.* IV.37). Gregory advised him to ignore the demand unless they had made a similar demand of his predecessor, Lawrence. Secundinus had to be reassured that the eastern churches upheld the council of Chalcedon (*ep.* IX.148). When Constantius wrote to Gregory that he dare not forward Gregory's letter to Queen Theodelinda because it mentioned the fifth council (II Constantinople, 553), Gregory agreed to drop the reference but, in a rare discussion, explicitly asserted that Justinian's council had done nothing that was in contradiction to the first four councils. Even people in communion with Rome showed similar symptoms of hyper-sensitivity when it came to Chalcedon. When the people of Ravenna complained that their bishop "did not honor Chalcedon enough," Gregory felt it necessary to reassure them (*ep.* VI.2). In such an atmosphere one can appreciate Gregory's frustration.[16]

The letter of the Irish monk Columban shows the extent of the problem that still persisted, even after Gregory's death. Columban's fifth letter is a plea to Rome that something be done to remedy the current *infamia cathedrae sancti Petri* (*ep.* 5.3). The sea is heavy and the Bark of Peter is taking on water, lamented Columban, with a bit of Gaelic exaggeration. Columban asserted that the Irish were well known for their veneration of Peter and Paul as well as their concern for orthodoxy, but he felt no hesitation in saying that Rome's reputation was very much in need of defense in the area of northern Italy where he was living (*ep.* 5.3: he specifically mentions the bishop of Como).

In the eyes of Columban, it was Rome's pastoral duty to act quickly to clarify the matter and settle it once and for all: *Vigilate ... pro ecclesiae pace* (*ep.* 5.4). The best way to make up for Vigilius' failure in vigilance (*ep.* 5.5) was to call a synod (*ep.* 5.10). The cloud of suspicion might then be lifted from the Chair of Peter. Your sons (the churches of the West) will be your judges, he warned, if you (Rome) support heretics (*ep.* 5.10). In Columban's view, Roman authority was not guaranteed *a priori* (*ep.* 5.11). The solution to the problem must be:

to meet and iron out disagreements; to agree on the things which are capable of being judged; to leave to God the things which cannot be settled. Both sides wish to defend the true faith. In closing, Columban assured the pope (Boniface IV, 608-615) that he was simply reporting what he had heard being said around him. His own confidence in Roman firmness remained unshaken (*ep.* 5.15). Columban's comments show little awareness of previous Roman efforts to restore unity. But his reporting of northern Italian opinions shows both that the opposition and hostility persisted and that precise knowledge of the origins of and reasons for the quarrel were growing ever harder to find.[17]

The initial problems of the western opponents of Justinian's intentions revolved very much more around a generalized anxiety that the truth of Chalcedon and the prestige of Leo were both being undermined than around a precise and detailed knowledge either of what had been done and said at Chalcedon or what Justinian intended. The doubters were fearful and wanted well enough left alone. Vigilius' vacillations compounded the harm done to Roman prestige. His detailed analyses in themselves did not convince either the easterners who were determined to condemn the Three Chapters nor the westerners who viewed any discussion of them as a betrayal of the sureties of the past. The popes after Vigilius almost never gave a detailed answer to their critics; but generalized assurances that all was well and that Roman orthodoxy remained unshaken and untainted carried little conviction. Gregory's detailed answers probably came too late (the third letter of Pelagius II).

Rome claimed that adjustments and revisions could be made within the assured doctrine of the past without threatening continuity and *firmitas*. Others were convinced that this was not done and that therefore continuity had been broken and Rome's reputation as a rock of certainty had been badly tarnished, if not destroyed.[18] Extolling the virtues of readiness to change and the humility of being ready to yield to a "better idea" was a far cry from Hormisdas' boast of never deviating from the established doctrine of the Fathers. It obviously did great harm to the Roman ideology insofar as it implied that Rome's previous positions might have been in terror. It posed serious questions about the continuity of orthodoxy.

As for I Peter 3.15 and Rome's new-found willingness to let its positions be examined on approval and analyzed by those who did not accept them without question could also be dangerous. It implied a lack of certainty or even outright rejection on the part of the questioners, things that Rome normally would not have admitted as possibilities. Can one envisage Gelasius cheerfully inviting people to look over his views and give him their reactions, inviting as it were rejection as well as acceptance? Clearly, then, non-Romans, including westerners, did not agree that the Roman position must be accepted and must be presumed to be correct simply because the Roman church and Roman bishop accepted and proclaimed it. Rome had usually been on the side of orthodoxy, but here and on a few other occasions it had fallen down on its perennial task and charism of *vigilantia*.

Finally, one might also ask about the efficacy of the *a priori* and continued assertion of Roman authority earlier. Despite it, dissenters on a variety of issues had continued to express their opposition on this or that problem. Even the greatest popes of the era, Leo for example, when dealing with doubters would offer a detailed explanation of their decisions while maintaining (for example, *ep*. 124.1 to the Palestinian monks) that the decision of Chalcedon and his tome should be sufficient reason to cease all opposition. Even the lordly Gelasius wrote lengthy and detailed explanations of his position to waverers. So, while some of the tactics of Pelagius I were novel and probably dangerous, it should not be forgotten that even those popes who made the boldest and broadest claims to authority seemed tacitly to grant that others would not automatically accept such claims.

Given the conviction of the northern Italians, neither detailed analyses nor general assurances would help. They would accept only a repudiation of Justinian's council and now that it had been accepted by Rome, more from coercion than conviction perhaps, to be sure, that could not be done without itself causing a break in continuity and being a repudiation of the actions of past popes. Only the passage of time and ongoing governmental pressure could ultimately restore unity even as the original complex issues became still more obscure and faded into a vague but bitter memory.

Conclusion

The history of the Papacy in Antiquity can be divided into two periods. The first is that before the time of Damasus, the period in which the documentary evidence, especially that coming from Roman sources, is very sketchy and episodic. The texts and historical cases surveyed and evaluated are subject to a variety of interpretations, some of which, to be sure, are more likely than others. Yet there is enough evidence of a Roman consciousness of its authority to show that the later firm and steady claims did not arise *ex nihilo* after 366. Non-Roman attitudes are another matter. There is no question of the esteem with which the Roman Christian community was held from an early moment in other parts of the Church. But such high regard could co-exist peacefully with a fierce determination to go one's own way and follow one's own traditions within the broad limits of the unity of the Church. And such unity was far from the uniformity we presume and witness today.

After 366, from the time of Damasus on, the Roman view of its own place in the Church is very clear. But once again, the question of the views of non-Romans must be considered. Thus acceptance, not only of Roman prestige but also of Roman authority, did not, as we have seen, even in the times of Leo and Gelasius, carry with it the presumption of automatic and unquestioning obedience to Roman directives. This rather steady growth in Roman prestige, augmented considerably by Roman support for the orthodox position in the Trinitarian and Christological disputes of the fourth and fifth centuries, reached its high point in the ancient church in the fifth century. Roman steadfastness contrasted sharply and favorably with the constant bickering, infighting and dubious theological positions held by some of the Eastern bishops, including those of the principal sees. Yet when Rome in the sixth century could no longer stand aloof and geographically distant from Eastern intrigues, the authority of the bishops of Rome, built up over the centuries, seemed to be undermined by the vacillations and equivocations of Pope Vigilius at the court of Justinian. Looking back over the sweep of history, we see that the troubles of the sixth century proved to be only a temporary obstruction and not a permanent setback for the rise of Roman authority.

The "care for all the churches" had made an early appearance among the concerns of the Roman Christians. But as this "solicitude" developed further, it took on more precise characteristics which have persisted and grown more pronounced. The earliest explicit attempts to urge uniformity based on Roman practice, now equated with the apostolic heritage, met with only indifferent success. But the principle remained and over the centuries, slowly but surely, persistence was rewarded.

In the realm of doctrine, the static views of the early anti-heretical authors continued to exercise a prevailing influence over Roman theory and practice. Yet, one might say paradoxically, not always with sufficient success. Regarded on a month to month or year to year basis, change was difficult to perceive. Rome was occasionally, after long efforts, prevailed upon to change, as in the case of addition of the *Filioque* clause to the creed. But once changes had been made, on the same grounds they were impossible to rescind. The principle that in practice each pope was bound by the decisions of his predecessors made papal decisions ever more momentous. So, closer to our own times, the nineteenth- and twentieth-century Marian definitions of what had been popular beliefs about Mary with no direct scriptural basis made future ecumenical efforts so much more difficult. A similar phenomenon may be seen more recently in the repeated condemnation of contraception. Thus decisions of the past have decisively closed off ever more possibilities for the future.

The Roman view and practice have been remarkably consistent. But is there a point where concern about the past becomes so obsessive as to be counterproductive for the future? If so, we are not likely to see any improvement of the situation. How do we distinguish living Tradition from dead traditionalism?

Tradition has led to a kind of scrupulosity about doctrine in favor of the past and ever more prejudicial to the future. Episcopal spirituality has repeatedly reminded bishops that they are responsible for the salvation of their flocks and that they will be so judged. Allied to this state of mind is the fascinating, if irritating, conversion of once progressive churchmen to conservatism once they have been elevated to the hierarchy. When asked about some of his earlier theological views, Cardinal Ratzinger is supposed to have replied that things look different from a position of pastoral responsibility.

John Mahoney, an English Jesuit who is currently a professor in the University of London, writes: "It is interesting to note, however, how in human affairs so admirable a quality as a strongly developed sense of responsibility for something, or for others, can at times transpose into something of a nervous, proprietorial attitude towards that thing and a suffocating attitude toward those others" (*The Making of Moral Theology*, 1987, p. 172). It might well be asked, for example, whether Rome's real problem with Liberation Theology revolves around fear of the use of "Marxist analysis" by such theologians or whether the basic anxiety does not rather reflect the fear that the Church hierarchy may suffer a loss of authority in the face of the "base communities" and the *Iglesia popular*.

Thus the old Roman fear that divergence of practice will lead to divergence of faith continues to show itself in a reluctance to loosen the strings and permit decentralization at this time in history when centralization is easier than ever to promote and administer. The long-sought goal of Roman theory has been achieved at last. Suspicion is cast on the value of episcopal conferences, and subsidiarity, it is suggested, applies only to civil society, not to the Church. The archaizing mistake (from the centralizers' point of view) made at Vatican

II is not likely to be repeated. The only direction before us points to a greater tightening of the leash.

As a problem in general and in all its aspects, authority is the ultimate stumbling block upon which all ecumenical efforts founder. I have often wondered whether John Henry Newman, whose long life (1801-1890) was evenly divided between Anglican and Roman periods, found a solution to that problem, a solution satisfactory at least to himself. He worried with good reason whether the Church of England had the strength and authority to resist the ever more pervasive threatening acids of modernity which even in the nineteenth century were beginning to eat away at Christian foundations. He looked to the Church of Rome as the only entity with sufficient authority and staying power to withstand the growing onslaught. But, once he had become a Roman Catholic in 1845, I wonder whether he did not experience more authoritarianism, if not authority, than he had bargained for (In addition, the state of the Roman Catholic Church in the late twentieth century raises the question of how well it in fact is able to withstand the movement of the all-engulfing amoeba of secularism.)

Is there a happy medium between freedom and authority? Newman himself came to the conclusion that his own vision of the Church of England as the *via media* existed nowhere except in his own mind, a paper creation. If there is a happy medium in some theologians' minds and books, how does it work in reality?

Endnotes

Chapter I

[1] H. Marot, "La Collégialité et le vocabulaire épiscopal du Ve au VIIe siécle," pp. 59-98 (especially pp. 94-5), in *La Collégialité épiscopale,* Unam Sanctam vol. 52 (Paris: Cerf, 1965).

[2] Several articles within the earlier collective volume *L'Épiscopat et l'Église universelle,* Unam Sanctam vol. 39 (Paris: Cerf, 1962) should be noted here: G. Dejaifve, "Primauté et collégialité au premier concile du Vatican," pp. 639-60; W. Dewan, "*Potestas vere episcopalis* au premier concile du Vatican," pp. 661-87; G. Thils, "*Potestas ordinaria,*" pp. 689-707; O. Rousseau, "La vraie valeur de l'Épiscopat dans l'Église d'aprés d'importants documents de 1875," pp. 709-36. Cf. also J. P. Torrell, *La Théologie de l'Épiscopat au premier concile du Vatican,* Unam Sanctam vol. 37 (Paris: Cerf, 1961).

[3] G. Alberigo and J. P. Jossua, eds., *The Reception of Vatican II.* Translated by Matthew O'Connell. (Washington: The Catholic University of America Press, 1987). (French original 1985) Especially: H. J. Pottmeyer, "A New Phase in the Reception of Vatican II: Twenty Years of Interpretation of the Council," pp. 27-43.

[4] Antonio Acerbi, *Due Ecclesiologie. Ecclesiologia giuridica ed ecclesiologia di communione nella 'lumen gentium'* (Bologna: Edizioni Dehoniane, 1975).

[5] Hierarchy of Truths: See *Mysterium ecclesiae #4* (USCC edition, p. 7) of 1973; U. Valeske, *Hierarchia veritatum* (Munich: Claudius Verlag, 1968).

[6] On William Chillingworth: Robert Orr, *Reason and Authority: The Thought of William Chillingworth* (Oxford: Clarendon Press, 1967), pp. 71-114.

[7] Hans Urs von Balthasar, *The Office of Peter and the Structure of the Church,* translated by A. Emery (San Francisco: Ignatius Press, 1986), p. 9. (German original: *Der antirömische Affekt,* 1974).

[8] *Michael Fighting,* Fall 1975 (Rougement, Québec). English language edition, #8.

[9] O. Cullmann, *Peter: Disciple, Apostle, Martyr,* translated by Floyd Filson (New York: Living Age Books, 1958) from the German original of 1952. For a critical comment from a Catholic, see: K. Hofstetter, "Das Petrusamt in der Kirche des 1.-2. Jahrhunderts: Jerusalem-Rom," in *Begegnung der Christen: Festschrift O, Karrer,* ed. Roesle-Cullmann (Frankfurt: Knecht, 1959), pp. 373-89.

[10] R. Brown, K. Donfried, and J. Reumann, editors, *Peter in the New Testament: A Collective Assessment by Protestant and Roman Catholic Scholars* (Minneapolis: Augsburg Press; New York: Paulist Press, 1973).

11Walter Bauer, *Orthodoxy and Heresy in Earliest Christianity,* edited by R. Kraft and G. Krodel, translated by members of the Philadelphia Seminar on Christian Origins from the second German edition of G. Strecker (Philadelphia: Fortress Press, 1971); German original 1934.

12Terence Smith, *Petrine Controversies in Early Christianity,* Wissenschaftliche Untersuchungen zum Neuen Testament, 2. Reihe, Bd. 15 (Tübingen: J. C. B. Mohr [Paul Siebeck], 1985).

13R. Pesch, *Simon-Petrus: Geschichte und Geschichtliche Bedeutung des ersten Jüngers Jesu Christi,* Päpste und Papsttum Band 15 (Stuttgart: Anton Hiersemann, 1980): see Norbert Brox, "Probleme einer Frühdatierung des Römischen Primats," *Kairos* 18 (1976), pp. 81-99, especially pp. 84-7.

14D. W. O'Connor, *Peter in Rome: The Literary, Liturgical and Archeological Evidence* (New York: Columbia University Press, 1969); G. Snyder, "Survey and 'New' Thesis on the Tomb of Peter," *Biblical Archeologist* 32 (1969), pp. 2-24; K. Heussi, *Die römische Petrustradition in kritische Sicht* (Tübingen: J. C. B. Mohr [Paul Siebeck], 1955); J. E. Walsh, *The Bones of St. Peter: The First Full Account of the Search for the Apostle's Body* (Garden City, New York,: Doubleday, 1982); G. Snyder, *Ante Pacem: Archeological Evidence of Church Life before Constantine* (Macon, Georgia: Mercer University Press, 1985), especially pp. 145-47.

15Eusebius, *Historia Ecclesiastica* II.25.7; cf. W. Rordorf, "Was heisst: Petrus und Paulus haben die Kirche in Rom 'gegründet'?" in *Unterwegs zur Einheit: Festschrift H. Stirnimann,* eds. J. Brantschen and P. Selvatico (Friebourg: University Press, 1980), pp. 609-16; Y. Congar, "S. Paul et l'autorité de l'Église romaine d'après la Tradition," *Studiorum Paulinorum Congressus internationalis catholicus 1961,* vol. 1, Analecta biblica 17 (Roma: Biblicum, 1963), pp. 491-516.

16A. M. Javierre, "Le théme de la succession des Apôtres dans la littérature chrétienne primitive," in *L'Épiscopat et l'Église universelle,* edited by Y. Congar and B. D. Dupuy, Unam Sanctam 39 (Paris: Cerf, 1962), pp. 171-221, especially pp. 188-90.

17Among many references to the question of the development of ministries in the local churches, see E. Schillebeeckx, *The Church with a Human Face* (New York: Crossroad, 1985), pp. 81-123. For a critique of the first edition of this work, see P. Grelot, *Église et ministéres* (Paris: Cerf, 1983). N. Mitchell, *Mission and Ministry: History and Theology of the Sacrament of Orders,* Message of the Sacraments 6 (Wilmington, Delaware: Michael Glazier, 1982). R. Brown, *Priest and Bishop* (New York: Paulist Press, 1970). A. Lemaire, *Les ministéres aux origines de l'Église: Naissance de la triple Hiérarchie: évéques, presbytres, diacres,* Lectio divina 68 (Paris: Cerf, 1971); A. Lemaire, *Les ministéres dans l'Église,* Croire et comprendre (Paris: Centurion, 1974). B. Cooke, *Ministry to Word and Sacrament: History and Theology* (Philadelphia: Fortress Press, 1976). P. Nautin, "L'Évolution des ministéres au IIe and au IIIe siécle," *Revue du Droit Canonique* 23 (1973), pp. 47-58.

18Hans Küng, *The Church* (New York: Sheed & Ward, 1968) (German original, 1967).

19J. Colson, *Les Fonctions ecclésiales aux deux premiers siécles* (Paris: DDB, 1956).

20On Ignatius, see William Schoedel, *Ignatius of Antioch,* Hermeneia series (Philadelphia: Fortress Press, 1985). On the dating and authenticity of Ignatius' letters, cf. R. Joly, *Le Dossier d'Ignace d'Antioche* (Bruxelles: Éditions de l'Université, 1979). J. Rius-Camps, *The Four Authentic Letters of Ignatius the Martyr,* Christianismos 2 (Rome: Oriental Institute, 1979). R. Weijenborg, *Les Lettres d'Ignace d'Antioche: Étude de critique littéraire et de théologie* (Leiden: Brill, 1969). M. P. Brown, *The*

Authentic Writings of Ignatius (Durham: Duke University Press, 1963). Virginia Corwin, *St. Ignatius and Christianity in Antioch* (New Haven: Yale University Press, 1960).

[21]Cf. Origen, *Contra Celsum*, III.10; R. J. Hoffman, *Celsus: On the True Doctrine: A Discourse against the Christians* (New York: Oxford University Press, 1987), p. 70; K. Pichler, *Streit um das Christentum*, Regensburger Studien zur Theologie, Bd. 23 (Bern: Peter Lang, 1980); Origen, *Contra Celsum* v. 63.

[22]Yves Congar, *La Tradition and les Traditions: Essai historique*, vol. 1 (Paris: Fayard, 1960), pp, 41-121; Robert Eno, *Teaching Authority in the Early Church*, Message of the Fathers of the Church 14 (Wilmington, Delaware: Michael Glazier, 1984), pp. 13-29; D. van den Eynde, *Les Normes de l'Enseignement chrétien dans la littérature patristique des trois premiers siècles* (Gembloux: Duculot, 1933).

[23]Tertullian, *CCl* 1.

[24]V. Grossi, "Regulae Fidei" in *Dizionario patristico e di Antichità cristiana (DPAC)* vol. 2, cc. 2981-82; A. Brekelmans, "Origin and Function of Creeds in the Early Church," *Concilium* vol. 1,6 (June, 1970), pp. 33-42; Hippolytus, *La Tradition apostolique de Saint Hippolyte: Essai de Reconstitution*, ed. by Bernard Botte, Liturgiewissenschaftliche Quellen und Forschungen, Heft 39 (Münster: Aschendorff, 1963), #21, pp. 48-51.

[25]On Montanism, see: Eusebius, *Hist. eccl.* v. 16-17.

[26]Apostolic sees: O. Kéramé, "Les chaires apostoliques et le role des Patriarcats dans l'Église," in Congar and Dupuy, eds., *L'Épiscopat et l'Église universelle*, pp. 261-278; East-West Differences: K. Lübeck, *Reichseinteilung und kirchliche Hierarchie des Orients bis zum Ausgange des vierten Jahrhunderts*, Kirchengeschichtliche Studien V, 4 (Münster: H. Schöningh, 1901); F. Dvornik, *Byzantium and the Roman Primacy*, (New York: Fordham University Press, 1966), chs. 1-2, pp. 27-58. (French original 1964).

[27]Peter Brown, *The Cult of the Saints: Its Rise and Function in Late Antiquity* (Chicago: University of Chicago Press, 1981).

[28]Raymond Brown and John Meier, *Antioch and Rome: New Testament Cradles of Catholic Christianity* (New York: Paulist Press, 1983), pp. 162-65.

[29]See now the important study of Peter Lampe, *Die stadtrömischen Christen in den ersten beiden Jahrhunderten*, Wissenschaftlichen Untersuchungen zum Neuen Testament, 2. Reihe, Bd. 18 (Tübingen: J. C. B. Mohr [Paul Siebeck], 1987), especially pp. 334-45.

Chapter II

[1]For the title, see Cyprian, *Ep.* 66.8.

[2]For the East on Peter, see *The Primacy of Peter in the Orthodox Church* (London: Faith Press, 1963), especially John Meyendorff, "St. Peter in Byzantine Theology," pp. 7-29; N. Koulomzine, "Peter's Place in the Early Church," pp. 111-134.

[3]On "Bishop Lists," see L. Koop, "Bischofsliste," *Reallexikon für Antike und Christentum (RAC)*, Bd. 2, cc. 407-415 (1954); A. diBerardino, "Liste episcopali," *DPAC* vol. 2, cc. 1971-1973.

[4]"*Episkope*," G. Kittel, *Theological Dictionary of the New Testament (TNDT)*, vol. 2, 606-08; "episkopos," 608-20, by H. Beyer (Grand Rapids: Eerdmans, 1964).

(German original *ca.* 1953). Raymond Brown, "*Episkope* and *episkopos:* The New Testament Evidence," *Theological Studies* 41 (1980), 322-338; the same article appeared in *Episkope and Episcopate in Ecumenical Perspective,* Faith and Order Paper 102. (Geneva: World Council of Churches, 1980), pp. 15-29. Also in that booklet, J. Zizioulas, "*Episkope* and *Episkopos* in the Early Church: A brief survey of the evidence," pp. 30-42.

⁵For the letter of Flora, see J. Stevenson, ed. *A New Eusebius,* rev. by W. H. C. Frend (London: SPCK, 1987), pp. 85-88; K. Koschorke, *Die Polemik der Gnostiker gegen das kirchliche Christentum* (Nag Hammadi Studies vol. 12) (Leiden: Brill, 1978).

⁶On Mark and Alexandria, see B. A. Pearson, "Earliest Christianity in Egypt: Some Observations," in *The Roots of Egyptian Christianity,* ed. B. Pearson and J. Goehring, Studies in Antiquity and Christianity (Philadelphia: Fortress Press, 1986), pp. 132-157, especially 137-145, "The Mark Legend;" E. R. Hardy, *Christian Egypt: Church and People: Christianity and Nationalism in the Patriarchate of Alexandria* (New York: Oxford University Press, 1952), pp. 11-13.

⁷On Hegesippus, see T. Halton, *Theologische Realenzyklopädie (TRE),* Bd. 14, 560-62.

⁸"Pre-eminent in love": see Johannes Quasten, *Patrology,* vol. 1 (Westminster, MD.: Newman Press, 1950), pp. 69-70; R. Staats, "Die martyrologische Begründung des Romprimates bei Ignatius von Antiochen,: *Zeitschrift für Theologie und Kirche* 73 (1976), pp. 461-70.

⁹On Clement of Rome, see *TRE* Bd. 8, pp. 113-121 (D. Powell); for a survey of scholarship since Harnack on this question, see J. Füllenbach, *Ecclesiastical Office and the Primacy of Rome: An Evaluation of Recent Theological Discussion of First Clement.* Studies in Christian Antiquity, 20. (Washington: The Catholic University of America Press, 1980).

¹⁰Tertullian, *De praescriptione haereticorum* 32, *CCL* 1.

¹¹Irenaeus, *Adversus Haereses* III.3.3; commentary and bibliography by L. Doutreleau and A. Rousseau, *Sources chrétiennes (SC)* 210 (Paris: Cerf, 1974), pp. 32-45; R. P. C. Hanson, "*Potentiorem principalitatem* in Irenaeus, *Adversus haereses* III.3.1," *Studia Patristica* 3, *Texte und Untersuchungen* Bd. 78 (Berlin: Akademie Verlag, 1961), pp. 366-69.

¹²Norbert Brox, "The Conflict between Anicetus and Polycarp," *Concilium* vol. 8 (January, 1972), pp. 32-45; "Tendenzen und Parteilichkeiten im Osterfeststreit des 2. Jahrhundert," *Zeitschrift für Kirchengeschichte* 83 (1972), pp. 291-324.

¹³For a dissenting view, cf. N. Zernov, "Eusebius and the Paschal Controversy at the End of the Second Century," *Church Quarterly Review* 116 (April 1933), pp. 24-41.

¹⁴G. LaPiana, "The Roman Church at the End of the Second Century," *Harvard Theological Review* 18 (1925), pp. 201-77. In general, see W. Huber, *Passa und Ostern,* Untersuchungen zur österfeier der alten Kirche (Berlin: A. Töpelmann, 1969), ch. 1, pp. 1-88.

¹⁵On Origen in general, see H. Crouzel, *Origen* (San Francisco: Harper & Row, 1989). For his ecclesiology, see H. J. Vogt, *Das Kirchenverständnis des Origenes,* Bonner Beiträge zur Kirchengeschichte, Bd. 4 (Köln: Böhlau Verlag, 1974), pp. 143ff.; Robert B. Eno, "Origen and the Church of Rome," *American Ecclesiastical Review* 167 (1973), pp. 41-50.

[16] *Pagans and Christians* (New York: A. Knopf, 1987), p. 408.

[17] Hippolytus, *La Tradition Apostolique de Saint Hippolyte:* Essai de reconstitution par Dom Bernard Botte, O.S.B. Liturgiewissenschaftliche Quellen und Forschungen, Heft 30. (Münster: Aschendorff, 1963).

[18] Hippolytus, *Refutatio omnium haeresium,* ed. P. Wendland, *GCS* 26: *Hippolytus Werke* III Bd. (Leipzig, 1916); new edition by Miroslav Marcovich, Patrische Texte und Studien, Bd. 25. (Berlin: de Gruyter, 1986).

[19] From the immense literature on Constantine, for a general survey: Peter Brown, *The World of Late Antiquity* (London: Thames and Hudson, 1971); for a rapid survey: A. H. M. Jones, *Constantine and the Conversion of Europe* (New York: Collier Books, 1962) (Original, 1948); a classic text: Norman Baynes, *Constantine the Great and the Christian Church,* second edition (Oxford University Press for the British Academy, 1972) (Original, Raleigh Lecture for 1930); a recent work: T. D. Barnes, *Constantine and Eusebius* (Cambridge, Mass.: Harvard University Press, 1981); *The New Empire of Diocletian and Constantine* (1982); St. Williams, *Diocletian and the Roman Recovery* (New York: Methuen, 1981).

[20] J. H. W. G. Liebeschuetz, *Continuity and Change in Roman Religion* (Oxford: Clarendon Press, 1979); A. Wardman, *Religion and Statecraft among the Romans* (Baltimore: Johns Hopkins University Press, 1982).

[21] R. Krautheimer, *Three Christian Capitals: Topography and Politics* (Berkeley: University of California Press, 1983), Rome: pp. 7-40.

[22] C. B. Coleman, *Constantine the Great and Christianity* (New York: AMS Press, 1968). (Original, Columbia University Press, 1914).

[23] On Constantine, see Johannes Straub, *Regeneratio Imperii: Aufsätze über Roms Kaisertum und Reich im Spiegel der heidnischen und christlichen Publizistik* (Darmstadt: Wissenschaftliche Buchgesellschaft, 1972), especially "Kaiser Konstantin als *episkopos ton ektos,*" pp. 119-133. (Original, "Constantine as *koinos episkopos*" *Dumbarton Oaks Papers* 23 (1967), pp. 37-55).

[24] H. J. Sieben, "Die Konzilidee des Eusebius von Caesarea oder der hellenistische Einfluss," in *Die Konzilsidee der Alten Kirche,* Konzilsgeschichte, Reihe B, Bd. 1 (Paderborn: Schöningh, 1979), pp. 424-465; P. L'Huillier, "Ecclesiology in the Canons of the First Nicene Council," *St. Vladimir's Seminary Theological Quarterly* 27 (1983), pp. 119-131.

[25] On Ossius, see V. DeClercq, *Ossius of Cordoba: A Contribution to the History of the Constantinian Period,* Studies in Christian Antiquity, vol. 13 (Washington: The Catholic University of America Press, 1954).

[26] On Athanasius and Eusebius, see V. Twomey, *Apostolikos Thronos:* The Primacy of Rome as Reflected in the *Church History* of Eusebius and the Historico-apologetic Writings of St. Athanasius the Great, Münsterische Beiträge zur Theologie, Bd. 49 (Münster: Aschendorff, 1982).

[27] V. Monachino, "Communio e Primato nella Controversia Ariana," *Archivum Historiae Pontificiae* 7 (1969), pp. 43-78; "Il Primato nella Controversia Ariana," *Miscellanea Historiae Pontificiae* 21 1959), pp. 17-89; W. Gessel, "Das primatiale Bewusstein Julius' I. im Lichte der Interaktionen zwischen der *Cathedra Petri* und den zeitgenössischen Synoden," in *Konzil und Papst:* Festschrift H. Tüchle, ed. G. Schwaiger, Historische Beiträge zur Frage der höchsten Gewalt in der Kirche (Paderborn: Schöningh, 1975), pp. 63-74; Charles Piétri, *Roma Christiana,* vol. I (Bibliothéque des Écoles françaises de Rome et d'Athénes, vol. 224) (Paris: de Boccard, 1976), pp. 187-237.

²⁸For the documents, see Shotwell and Loomis, eds., *The See of Peter* (New York: Columbia University Press, 1927; repr. 1963), pp. 503-516. On the Council of Sardica, see H. Hess, *The Canons of the Council of Sardica, A.D. 343: A Landmark in the development of Canon Law* (Oxford: Clarendon Press, 1958); Leslie Barnard, *The Council of Sardica 343* (Sofia: Synodal Press, 1983); M. Wojtowytsch, *Papsttum und Konzile von der Anfängen bis zu Leo I. (440-461): Studien zur Entstehung der überordnung des Papstes über Konzile,* Päpste und Papsttum Bd. 17 (Stuttgart: A. Hiersemann, 1981), Nicaea: pp. 82-89; Julius et al.: pp. 89-105; Sardica: pp. 106-16; H. Brennecke, "Rom und das dritte Kanon von Sardika (342)," *Zeitschrift der Savigny-Stiftung für Rechtsgeschichte (Kan. Abt.)* 69 (1983), pp. 15-42; H. J. Sieben, "*Sanctissimi Petri Apostoli memoriam honoremus:* Die Sardicensischen Appellationskanones im Wandel der Geschichte," *Theologie und Philosophie* 58 (1983), pp. 501-34.

²⁹On Constantius and the Western Church, see R. Klein, *Constantius II. und die christliche Kirche* (Darmstadt: Wissenschaftliche Buchgesellschaft, 1971).

³⁰On Liberius, see Piétri, *op. cit.,* pp. 237-68.

Chapter III

¹W. Marschall, *Karthago und Rom: Die Stellung der nordafrikanischen Kirche zum Apostolischen Stuhl in Rom.* Päpste und Papsttum Bd. 1 (Stuttgart: A. Hiersemann, 1971).

²On Tertullian, see T. D. Barnes, *Tertullian: An Historical and Literary Study* (Oxford: Clarendon Press, 1971); on Western and especially North African ecclesiology, see Robert Evans, *One and Holy: the Church in Latin Patristic Thought* (London: SPCK, 1972).

³Tertullian, *De praescriptione haereticorum,* CCL 1; SC 46 (1957).

⁴As an example of an argument over a single text, see Gérard Poupon, "Tertullien et le privilége de Pierre (Note sur *De pudicitia* 21.9-10," *Revue des études Augustiniennes* 32 [1986], pp. 142-144).

⁵P. Stockmeier, "Die übernahme des Pontifex-Titels im spätantiken Christentum," in *Konzil und Papst,* pp. 75-84; Yves Congar, "Titres donnés au Pape," *Concilium* 108 (1975), pp. 55-64, especially pp. 62-64.

⁶On Cyprian, see M. Sage, *Cyprian* (Cambridge, Mass.: Philadelphia Patristic Foundation, 1975); P. Hinchliff, *Cyprian of Carthage and the Unity of the Christian Church* (London: Chapman, 1974); A. Davids, "One or None: Cyprian on the Church and Tradition," *Concilium* vol. 1, #8 (January 1972), pp. 46-52.

⁷*De lapsis et De unitate ecclesiae,* ed. by M. Bévénot, CCL 3 and Oxford Early Christian Texts. *Epistolae:* Latin: Ed. Budé in 2 vols., ep. 8 Bayard, pp. 19-21. English translation only by G. W. Clarke, *Ancient Christian Writers* (ACW) 43, 44, 46, 47 (New York: Newman Press, 1984-89).

⁸*Opera* in CCL 4; see A. Demoustier, "Épiscopat et union á Rome selon St. Cyprien," *Recherches de Science religieuse* 52 (1964), pp. 337-368; "L'Ontologie de l'Église selon St. Cyprien," *RSR* 52 (1964), pp. 554-588; H. Gülzow, *Cyprian und Novatian* (Tübingen: J. C. M. Mohr [Paul Siebeck], 1975).

⁹H. Koch, "*Cathedra Petri:* Neue Untersuchungen über die Anfánge der Primatsidee," *Zeitschrift für Neutestamentliche Wissenschaft,* Beiheft 11 (Giessen: A. Töpelmann, 1930); Cyprian, *ep.* 33.1, Bayard p. 84; Cyprian, *ep.* 43.5, Bayard p. 107.

¹⁰*De unitate* 4, 6, 12; CCL 3.251-52; 253; 258; *ep.* 73.21, Bayard p. 275; *ep.* 66.8, Bayard p. 226.

¹¹*Ep.* 30.1, Bayard p. 71; *ep.* 68.1, Bayard pp. 234-35; *ep.* 52.2, Bayard p. 126.

¹²*Ep.* 48.3, Bayard, p. 118; *ep.* 59.14, Bayard p. 183.

¹³M. Sotomayer y Muro, "La Iglesia en la España romana, El caso de Basilides y Marcial," in *Historia de la Iglesia en España*, ed. R. Garcia Villoslada (Madrid: Biblioteca de Autores cristianos, 1979), pp. 124-128.

¹⁴A study of the choosing of bishops according to Cyprian: T. Osawa, *Das Bischofseinsetzungsverfahren bei Cyprian: Historische Untersuchungen zu den Begriffen iudicium, suffragium, testimonium, consensus* (Bern: Peter Lang, 1983); *ep.* 67.5, Bayard p. 231; *ep.* 68.3, Bayard p. 236; *ep.* 68.5, Bayard p. 238; *ep.* 66.8, Bayard p. 226.

¹⁵*Ep.* 69.7, Bayard p. 244; *ep.* 71, Bayard pp. 256-59; on the rebaptism controversy, see B. Neunheuser, *Baptism and Confirmation* (New York: Herder & Herder, 1964), pp. 99-106.

¹⁶*Ep.* 74.1, Bayard p. 279; *ep.* 74.9, Bayard pp. 285-86; *ep.* 75.25, Bayard pp. 307-8; *ep.* 75.2-3, Bayard pp. 289-90; *ep.* 75.17, Bayard p. 301; on Firmilian of Caesarea, see *DPAC* 1, cc. 1378-79 (P. Nautin).

¹⁷*Ep.* 75.6, Bayard p. 293; *ep.* 75.25, Bayard p. 307; *ep.* 75.17, Bayard pp. 301-2; *ep.* 75.6, Bayard p. 293; *ep.* 75.25, Bayard p. 307-8.

¹⁸On the martyrdom of Cyprian, see *Acta proconsularia*, edited by Herbert Musurillo, S.J., *The Acts of the Christian Martyrs*, Oxford Early Christian Texts (Oxford: Clarendon Press, 1972), pp. 168-175; *Sententiae episcoporum*, *CSEL* 3, p. 435.

¹⁹On Donatism, see W. H. C. Frend, *The Donatist Church: A movement of protest in Roman North Africa*, first edition (Oxford: Clarendon Press, 1952); Paul Monceaux, *Histoire littéraire de l'Afrique chrétienne depuis les origines jusqu'à l'invasion arabe*, vol. 4: "Le Donatisme," (Bruxelles: Culture et Civilisation, 1912: repr. 1966).

²⁰On *traditio*, see B. Kriegbaum, *Kirche der Traditoren oder Kirche der Märtyrer: Die Vorgeschichte des Donatismus*. Innsbrucker Theologische Studien Bd. 16 (Innsbruck: Tyrolia Verlag, 1986).

²¹On the Council of Arles of 314, see *DPAC* I, cc. 365-66 (C. Munier); *Conciles gaulois du IVe siécle*, edited by J. Gaudemet, *SC* 241, pp. 35-67.

²²On Optatus, his works are edited by C. Ziwsa, *CSEL* 26; English translation by O. R. Vassall-Phillips (London: Longmans, Green, 1917); *DPAC* vol. II, cc. 2549-2552 (F. Scorza Barcellona); Monceaux, vol. 5: *Saint Optat et les premiers écrivains Donatistes* (1920).

²³The bibliography on Augustine is immense. Three basic modern works are Peter Brown, *Augustine of Hippo* (Berkeley: University of California Press, 1967); F. van der Meer, *Augustine the Bishop: The Life and Work of a Father of the Church* (New York: Sheed & Ward, 1961) (Dutch original, 1947); a brief work by Henry Chadwick, *Augustine*, Past Masters series (Oxford: Oxford University Press, 1986).

On Augustine's ecclesiology, see F. Hofmann, *Der Kirchenbegriff des Hl. Augustinus in seinem Grundlagen und in seinem Entwicklung* (Reprint: Münster: Stenderhoff, 1978) (Original, Munich, 1933); J. Ratzinger, *Volk und Haus Gottes in Augustins Lehre von der Kirche*, Münchener Theologische Studien, II. Systematische

Abteilung, Bd. 7 (Munich: Karl Zink Verlag, 1954). Augustine and Rome, see Robert B. Eno, "Doctrinal Authority in Augustine," *Augustinian Studies* 12 (1981), pp. 133-172; H. M. Klinkenberg, *"Unus Petrus-Generalitas Ecclesiae* bei Augustinus, Zum Problem von Vielheit und Einheit," in *Miscellanea Mediaevalia* Bd. 5, "Universalismus und Partikularismus im Mittelatler" (Berlin: de Gruyter, 1968), pp. 216-242; F. Hofmann, "Die Bedeutung der Konzilien für die kirchliche Lehrentwicklung nach dem H1. Augustinus," in *Kirche und überlieferung: Festschrift Geiselmann,* ed. J. Betz & H. Fries (Freiburg: Herder, 1960), pp. 81-89; Karl Baus, "Wesen und Funktion der apostolischen Sukzession in der Sicht des h1. Augustinus," in *Ekklesia: Festschrift Bf. Wehr* (Trier: Paulinus Verlag, 1962), pp. 137-148.

[24]Augustine, *contra epistolam Fundamenti* IV.5, *Bibliothéque Augustinienne* 17.396 (BA) (Paris: DDB): *ep.* 53.2, *CSEL* 34/2, pp. 153-54; *Psalmus contra partem Donati,* vv. 236-39, *BA 28.184; Contra litteras Petiliani, BA* 30.382, 384; *Retractationes, BA* 12.400.

[25]*Sermo guelf.* 16.2, *Miscellanea Agostiniana* vol. 1.493; *sermo* 245.5, *PL* 38.1153; *sermo* 77.8, *PL* 38.486-87.

[26]On Pelagius, see a pioneering study by G. de Plinval, *Pélage: ses écrits, sa vie et sa réforme* (Lausanne: Payot, 1943); Robert F. Evans, *Pelagius: Inquiries and Reappraisals* (New York: Seabury Press, 1968); Augustinianum-Johannes Quasten, *Patrology,* vol. 4, pp. 465-86; G. Greshake, *Gnade als konkrete Freiheit: Eine Untersuchung zur Gnadenlehre des Pelagius* (Mainz: Matthias Grünewald, 1972); O. Wermelinger, *Rom und Pelagius: Die theologische Position der römischen Bischöfe im Pelagianischen Streit in den Jahren 411-412,* Päpste und Papsttum Bd. 7 (Stuttgart: A. Hiersemann, 1975).

[27]Augustine, *Ep.* 175.2, *CSEL* 44.655; *ep.* 177.19, *CSEL* 44.688; *ep.* 181.1, *CSEL* 44.702; *ep.* 182.2, *CSEL* 44.717.

[28]*Ep.* 181.1, *CSEL* 44.703; *sermo* 131.10, *PL* 38.734; Zosimus, *ep.* 12.1, *JW* 342 ("Quamvis patrum") *PL* 20.676-77.

[29]On Julian of Eclanum, see *DPAC* II, 1609-11 (V. Grossi); Augustinianum-J. Quasten, *Patrology,* vol. 4, pp. 487-92.

[30]Augustine, *De peccato originali* VII.8, *BA* 22.168, 170; *Contra duas epistolas Pelagianorum* II.III.5, *BA* 23.410; *Contra Julianum* VI.37, *PL* 44.

[31]On the Apiarius case, see *Concilia Africae, CCL* 149.79-149, Codex Apiarii causae, ed. C. Munier; cf. W. Marschall, *op. cit.,* pp. 161-203.

[32]Epistle of the Council of Carthage to Pope Boniface in *PL* 20.752.

[33]On the case of Antoninus of Fussala, see Augustine, *ep.* 209 to Pope Celestine, *CSEL* 57.347-353; *ep.* 20*, *CSEL* 88.94-112; *Les lettres de St. Augustin découvertes par Johannes Divjak,* Paris Colloquium of September 1982 (Paris: Études Augustiniennes, 1983); W. H. C. Frend, "Fussala, Augustine's Crisis of Credibility: *ep.* 20*," pp. 251-265; S. Lancel, "L'Affaire d'Antoninus de Fussala: pays, choses et gens de la Numidie d'Hippone saisis dans la durée d'une procédure d'enquête episcopale," pp. 267-285; C. Munier, "La Question des appels à Rome d'après la lettre 20* d'Augustin," pp. 287-299.

[34]"Optaremus," *PL* 50.423.

[35]C. Munier, "La Tradition littéraire des dossiers africains," *Revue de Droit canonique* 29 (1979), 41-52; "Un canon inédit du XXe Concile de Carthage: "Ut nullus ad Romanam ecclesiam audeat appellare'," *Revue des Sciences religieuses* 40 (1966), pp. 113-126.

[36]On Donatist clergy, see Rémi Crespin, *Ministère et Sainteté: Pastorale du clergé et solution de la crise donatiste dans la vie et la doctrine de St. Augustin,* esp. ch. 2: "Aurelius, primat de Carthage: nouvelles mésures concernant les clercs donatistes et leur conversion," (Paris: Études Augustiniennes, 1965), pp. 53-76.

[37]*Ep.* 22*.11, *CSEL* 88.119; *ep.* 23*A.5, *CSEL* 88.124; *ep.* 9*.1, *CSEL* 88.43. See also in the Paris colloquium volume, C. Piétri, "Les lettres nouvelles et leurs témoignages sur l'histoire de l'Église romaine et de ses rélations avec l'Afrique," pp. 343-354.

[38]On councils, see F. Hofmann, *op. cit.;* also Augustine, *De baptismo* I.VII,9, *BA* 29.78; II.III.4, *BA* 29.132, 134.

Chapter IV

[1]On Ambrose, see F. H. Dudden, *The Life and Times of Saint Ambrose,* 2 vols. (Oxford: Clarendon Press, 1935); Angelo Paredi, *Saint Ambrose: His Life and Times,* trans. J. Costello (Notre Dame, Ind.: University of Notre Dame Press, 1964). Bibliography: *Cento Anni di bibliografia ambrogiana 1874-1974,* Studia patristica mediolanensia 11 (Milano: Vita e Pensiero, 1981).

[2]Paulinus of Milan, *Vita Ambrosii* 38, *PL* 14.40 (Sollicitudo omnium ecclesiarum).

[3]On Aquileia, see *Aquileia e Milano,* Antichitá Altoadriatiche IV (Udine: Arti Grafiche Friulane, 1973); *Atti del Colloquio internazionale sul concilio di Aquileia del 381 A.A. 21* (1981).

[4]Henry Chadwick, *Priscillian of Avila: The Occult and the Charismatic in the Early Church* (Oxford: Clarendon Press, 1976).

[5]*De excessu fratris* I.47, *CSEL* 73.235; Council of Aquileia, *ep.* 11.4, *PL* 16.986B.

[6]*De incarnationis Domini sacramento* 32, *CSEL* 79.239.

[7]*De sacramentis* III.1.5, *CSEL* 73.40; on foot washing in Ambrose, see Pier Franco Beatrice, *La Lavanda dei Piedi: Contributo alla Storia delle antiche liturgie cristiane.* Bibliotheca 'Ephemerides Liturgicae.' Subsidia 28. (Roma: Edizioni liturgiche, 1983), chapter 5 on Ambrose, pp. 103-127.

[8]"Ubi Petrus, ibi Ecclesia." Cf. Roger Gryson, *Le Prêtre selon Saint Ambroise* (Louvain: édition orientaliste, 1968), pp. 215-217, and, in general, chapter 4, pp. 149-218.

[9]On Jerome, see J. N. D. Kelly, *Jerome: His Life, Writings, and Controversies* (London: Duckworth, 1975); Y. Bodin, *St. Jérome et l'Église,* Théologie historique, vol. 6 (Paris: Beauchesne, 1966), especially pp. 204-215; K. Sugano, *Das Rombild des Hieronymus* (Bern: Peter Lang, 1983).

[10]*Ep.* 15.2, Budé, ed. J. Labourt, vol. 1, p. 47.

[11]*Adversus Jovinianum* II.37-38, *PL* 23.337; *ep.* 127.9, Labourt ed., vol. 7, p. 144.

Chapter V

[1]Charles Pietri, *Roma Christiana* 2 vols.; *Saecularia Damasiana,* Studi di Antichità cristiana, vol. 39 (Roma: Pont. Inst. di Arch. crist., 1985).

[2]Ammianus Marcellinus, translated by J. C. Rolfe, Loeb Classical Library, vol. 3 (Cambridge, Mass.: Harvard University Press, 1939), pp. 18-21.

³Gregory Nazianzus, *Oratio* 42.24, *PG* 36; cf. John Meyendorff, "The Council of 381 and the Primacy of Constantinople," in *Catholicity and the Church* (New York: St. Vladimir's Seminary Press, 1983), pp. 121-142.

⁴The Roman Council of 382 = (part of the) *Decretum Gelasianum.* The "Decree" is generally regarded today as a compilation of the early sixth century from Italy (not Rome) or Southern Gaul. Many of the materials come from an earlier period but the authenticity of this particular section is not beyond dispute. See *DPAC* I.901-02 (E. Peretto).

⁵On Popes and Councils, see the references already given to: Wojtowytsch; Tüchle *Festschrift;* W. de Vries, *Orient et Occident: Les Structures ecclésiales vues dans l'histoire des sept premiers conciles oecuméniques* (Paris: Cerf, 1974). (Most of the articles had been published separately in German between 1967 and 1973).

⁶Siricius, *ep.* 1.2, *PL* 13.1133, Jaffé-Wattenbach (JW) 255; Damasus, *ep.* 1, *PL* 13, 348-49, JW 232; Innocent, *ep.* 5, *PL* 20.495A, JW 288; *ep.* 7.3, *PL* 29, 505, JW 294.

⁷Siricius, *ep.* 1.8.12, *PL* 13.1142, JW 255; *ep.* 5.4, *PL* 13.1162, JW 258; *ep.* 7.4, *PL* 13.1171, JW 260; Innocent, *ep.* 2.1, *PL* 20.469, JW 286; Siricius, *ep.* 1.20, *PL* 13.1146, JW 255; Innocent, *ep.* 24.4.3, *PL* 20.551, JW 310; *ep.* 29, *PL* 20, JW 321.

⁸Siricius, *ep.* 1.7.8, *PL* 13.1138, JW 255; *ep.* 6.1, *PL* 13.1164, JW 263, Sixtus, *ep.* 1.6, *Pl* 50.587, JW 389; Innocent, *ep.* 35, *PL* 20.601-02, JW 325; Celestine, *ep.* 20.1, *PL* 50.511-13; Innocent, *ep.* 2.17, *PL* 20.481, JW 286; Celestine, *ep.* 24.3, *PL* 50.548, JW 387; Anastasius, *ep.* 1.5, *PL* 20.72, JW 282.

⁹Siricius, *ep.* 4, *PL* 13.1149, JW 257; Boniface, *ep.* 4.2, *PL* 20.760, JW 350; *ep.* 5.1, *PL* 20.762, JW 351; Innocent, *ep.* 1, *PL* 20.464-65, JW 285; *ep.* 32, *PL* 20.597, JW 324; Boniface, *ep.* 5.2, *PL* 20.762, JW 351; Celestine, *ep.* 11.4, *PL* 50.463, JW 372; *ep.* 14.7, *PL* 50.495-98, JW 375.

¹⁰Celestine, *ep.* 17, *PL* 50.503, JW 378; *ep.* 18.5, *PL* 50.511, JW 379; Zosimus, *ep.* 1.1, *PL* 20.642-43, JW 328; *ep.* 10, *PL* 20.673-74, JW 340; Boniface, *ep.* 15.1, *PL* 20.779, JW 365; Damasus, decree to the bishops of Gaul, *PL* 13.1182, JW post 285; Siricius, *ep.* 1.15.20, *PL* 13.1146, JW 255; Innocent, *ep.* 17.1, *PL* 20.527, JW 303; *ep.* 6, *PL* 20.495, JW 293; Boniface, *ep.* 5.4, *PL* 20.763, JW 351; Innocent, *ep.* 2.5, *PL* 20.472-73, JW 286.

¹¹Innocent, *ep.* 30, *CSEL* 44.715, JW 322; Zosimus, *ep.* 9.1-2, *PL* 20.670-71, JW 339; Innocent, *ep.* 37.1-2, *PL* 20.603, JW 314; Boniface, *ep.* 4.1, *PL* 20.760, JW 350.

¹²Anastasius, *ep.* 2.2, *PL* 20.75, *JW* 276; Innocent, *ep.* 29.1, *CSEL* 44.702, *JW* 321; Zosimus, *ep.* 15.1, *PL* 20.681, *JW* 347; Celestine, *ep.* 13.9, *PL* 50.483, *JW* 374; Siricius, *ep.* 1.2.3, *PL* 13.1135-36, *JW* 255; Sixtus, *ep.* 10.4, *PL* 50.618, *JW* 396; Boniface, *ep.* 15.6, *PL* 20.782, *JW* 365.

¹³Zosimus, *ep.* 12.1, *PL* 20.676-77, JW 342; Boniface, *ep.* 13.2, *PL* 20.776, JW 363; *ep.* 15.5, *PL* 20.781-82, JW 365; Cyprian, *ep.* 59.14, ed. Bayard p. 183; Siricius, *ep.* 5.1, *PL* 13.1155, JW 258; Innocent, *ep.* 2.2, *PL* 20.470, JW 286.

¹⁴Innocent, *ep.* 29.1, *CSEL* 44.702, JW 321; *ep.* 23, *PL* 20.546, JW 309; *ep.* 24.1, *PL* 20.547-48, JW 310; Damasus, *ep.* 7, *PL* 13.370, JW 234; Council of Arles.

¹⁵Siricius, *ep.* 1.1, *PL* 13.1132-33, JW 235; Boniface, *ep.* 5.1, *PL* 20.762, JW 351; *ep.* 15.4, *PL* 20.781, JW 365; Innocent, *ep.* 17.7.14, *PL* 20.536, JW 303; Boniface, *ep.* 15.7, *PL* 20.783-84, JW 365; Celestine, *ep.* 22.6, *PL* 50.541, JW 385; Sixtus, *ep.* 6.5, *PL* 50.609, JW 392.

¹⁶Innocent, *ep.* 17.5.9, *PL* 20.532, JW 303.

¹⁷Innocent, *ep.* 25.1-2, Cabié, ed., pp. 18, 20, JW 311.

[18]Zosimus, *ep.* 1.3.2, *PL* 20.644-45, JW 328; *ep.* 6.2, *PL* 20.667-78, JW 332; *ep.* 5, *PL* 20.665-66, JW 334; *ep.* 2.8, *PL* 20.653-54, JW 329; *ep.* 2.1, *PL* 20.649, JW 329; Boniface, *ep.* 14.2, 4, *PL* 20.777-78, JW 364; Innocent, *ep.* 13.2, *PL* 20.515-16, JW 300; *ep.* 3, *PL* 20.486, JW 292; Siricius, *ep.* 5.1, *PL* 13.1156, JW 258.

[19]Innocent, *ep.* 2.2, *PL* 20.471, JW 286; *ep.* 25, Cabié, ed., p. 20, JW 311; Celestine, *ep.* 4.5, *PL* 50.434, JW 369; *ep.* 5.3, *PL* 50.437, JW 371; Innocent, *ep.* 2.2, *PL* 20.470, JW 286; Celestine, *ep.* 3, *PL* 50.428, JW 366; Eusebius, *Hist. eccl.* V.24.16, Loeb I.510; Tertullian, *Adversus Praxean* 1, *CCL* 2.1159.

[20]Innocent, *ep.* 1, *PL* 20.465, JW 285; *ep.* 14, *PL* 20.517, JW 301; Sixtus, *ep.* 1.2, *PL* 50.585, JW 389; Celestine, *ep.* 14.2, *PL* 50.487, JW 375; *ep.* 19.2, *PL* 50.511-12, JW 380; Damasus, Decree to the bishops of Gaul, *PL* 13.1188, *CPL* 1632, JW post 285; Innocent, *ep.* 2.17, *PL* 20.481, JW 286.

Chapter VI

[1]On Leo the Great, see T. G. Jalland, *The Life and Times of St. Leo the Great* (London: SPCK, 1941); P. McShane, *La Romanitas et le Pape Léon le Grand: L'Apport culturel des institutions impériales á la formation des structures ecclésiastiques*, Recherches-Théologie 24 (Montréal: Bellarmin, 1979).

[2]Leo, *sermo* 4.2, *CCL* 138.18; *sermo* 82.1, 3, *CCL* 138A.509.

[3]Leo, *sermo* 82.3, *CCL* 138A.512; *sermo* 62.2, *CCL* 138A.378; *sermo* 5.2, *CCL* 138.23; *sermo* 5.4, *CCL* 138.24; *sermo* 4.4, *CCL* 138.21; *ep.* 25.2 (Peter Chrysologus), *PL* 54.743.

[4]Leo, *ep.* 14.11, *PL* 54.676, JW 411; *sermo* 4.3, *CCL* 138.19.

[5]Leo, *ep.* 6.2, *PL* 54.617-18, JW 404; *ep.* 5.6, *PL* 54.616, JW 403; *ep.* 6.1, *PL* 54.617, JW 404; *ep.* 5.2, *PL* 54.615, JW 403; *ep.* 14.1, *PL* 54.668-69, JW 411; *sermo* 5.5, *CCL* 138.24-25; *ep.* 14.1, *PL* 54.671, JW 411; *ep.* 4.2, 5, *PL* 54.612-14, JW 402.

[6]Leo, *ep.* 16.1, 7, *PL* 54.696, 702-03, JW 414; *ep.* 10.1, *PL* 54.629, JW 407; *ep.* 68.1, *PL* 54.889; *ep.* 99.5, *PL* 54.968.

[7]Leo, *ep.* 65.2, *PL* 54.880-81; *ep.* 33.1, *PL* 54.797, JW 427; *epp.* 55-56, e.g., 56, *PL* 54.861; *ep.* 120.1-2, *PL* 54.1047-49, JW 496; the authenticity of *ep.* 120 is disputed.

[8]Leo, *ep.* 119.3, *PL* 54.1043, JW 495; *ep.* 130.3, *PL* 54.1080, JW 506; *ep.* 5.2, *PL* 54.615, JW 403; *sermo* 5.4, *CCL* 138.24; *ep.* 12.1, *PL* 54.646, JW 408.

[9]Leo, *ep.* 61.1, *PL* 54.874, JW 449; *ep.* 75.1, *PL* 54.902, JW 457; *ep.* 124.1, *PL* 54.1062-63, JW 500; *ep.* 123.1, *PL* 54.1060, JW 499; *ep.* 120.6, *PL* 54.1054, JW 496; *sermo* 3.2, 3, *CCL* 138.11-13; *ep.* 5.4, *CCL* 138.24; *sermo* 83.1, 3, *CCL* 138A.519, 521; *ep.* 12.13, *PL* 54.656, JW 408.

[10]Leo, *ep.* 1.2, *PL* 54.594, JW 398; *ep.* 6.4, *PL* 54.618, JW 404; *ep.* 90.2, *PL* 54.933-34, JW 470; *ep.* 94, *PL* 54.941, JW 474; *ep.* 102.4, *PL* 54.987, JW 479; *ep.* 120.5, *PL* 54.1053-54, JW 496; *ep.* 120.4, *PL* 54.1052-53, JW 496; *ep.* 163, *PL* 54.1147, JW 540; *ep.* 116.2, *PL* 54.1036, JW 492; *ep.* 117.1, *PL* 54.1037, JW 493; *ep.* 160.2, *PL* 54.1142, JW 537.

[11]Leo, *ep.* 162.1, *PL* 54.1144, JW 539; for the interpretation *episcopus* as *speculator* see the address of Christine Mohrmann to the Fifth International Patristic Conference, Oxford, September 1967.

[12]Leo, *ep.* 4, prol., *PL* 54.610, JW 402; *ep.* 6.1, *PL* 54.617, JW 404.

¹³Leo, *ep.* 14.11, *PL* 54.675, JW 411; *ep.* 16.1, *PL* 54.695-96, JW 414; *ep.* 99.4, *PL* 54.968; *ep.* 79.2, *PL* 54.911-12, JW 459; *ep.* 83.2, *PL* 54.920, JW 463.

¹⁴Leo, *ep.* 85.1, *PL* 54.922, JW 465; *ep.* 119.3, *PL* 54.1042-43, JW 495; *ep.* 120.6, *PL* 54.1054, JW 496; *ep.* 165.1, *PL* 54.1155, JW 542; *ep.* 10.2, *PL* 54.629, JW 407; *ep.* 13.1, *PL* 54.664, JW 409; *ep.* 66.2, *PL* 54.884-85, JW 450.

¹⁵Leo, *ep.* 82.1, *PL* 54.918, JW 462; *ep.* 10.9, *PL* 54.635-36, JW 407; *ep.* 106.5, *PL* 54.1005, 1007, JW 483; *ep.* 104.3, *PL* 54.993, 995, JW 481; *ep.* 105.2, *PL* 54.999, JW 482; *ep.* 106.2, *PL* 54.1003, JW 483; *ep.* 115.1, *PL* 54.1033, JW 491; *ep.* 119.2, *PL* 54.1042, JW 495.

¹⁶Leo, *ep.* 129.3, *PL* 54.1077, JW 505; *ep.* 114.2, *PL* 54.1031, JW 490; *ep.* 110, *PL* 54.1018, 1020; *ep.* 157.3, *PL* 54.1133, JW 534; *ep.* 164.3, *PL* 54.1151, JW 541; *ep.* 9, *PL* 54.625, JW 406.

¹⁷Leo, *ep.* 102.4, *PL* 54.987, JW 479; *ep.* 9.1, *PL* 54.625, JW 406; *ep.* 138, *PL* 54.1101-02, JW 512; *ep.* 16.2, *PL* 54.698, JW 414; *sermo* 79.1, *CCL* 138A.498; *ep.* 19.1, *PL* 54.709-10, JW 417; *ep.* 6.4, *PL* 54.618, JW 404; *ep.* 159.7, *PL* 54.1139-40, JW 536; *ep.* 96, *PL* 54.945, JW 477; *ep.* 119.6, *PL* 54.1046, JW 495.

¹⁸Leo, *ep.* 119.2, *PL* 54.1042, JW 495; *ep.* 102.4, *PL* 54.987, JW 479; *ep.* 61.2, *PL* 54.875, JW 449; *sermo* 2.2, *CCL* 138.8-9; *sermo* 3.3-4, *CCL* 138.13-15; *sermo* 5.1, *CCL* 138.22; *sermo* 82.7, *CCL*138A.517; see W. de Vries, *Orient et Occident*.

¹⁹Leo, *ep.* 44.1, *PL* 54.829, JW 438.

²⁰Leo, *ep.* 33.1, 2, *PL* 54.797, 799, JW 427.

²¹Leo, *ep.* 44.2, *PL* 54.829, JW 438; *ep.* 45.2, *PL* 54.833, 835, JW 439; *ep.* 54, *PL* 54.856, JW 445; *ep.* 69, *PL* 54.892, JW 452; *ep.* 36, *PL* 54.809-11, JW 430; *ep.* 37, *PL* 54.811-12, JW 431; *ep.* 73, *PL* 54.899; *ep.* 76, *PL* 54.904; *ep.* 89, *PL* 54.930, JW 469; *ep.* 90.1, *PL* 54.932-33, JW 470; *ep.* 93.1-2, *PL* 54.937, 939, JW 473.

²²Leo, *ep.* 100, *PL* 54.971; *ep.* 104.1, *PL* 54.991, JW 481; *ep.* 102.4, *PL* 54.987, JW 479; *ep.* 120.4, *PL* 54.1052, JW 496; *ep.* 103, *PL* 54.992, JW 480; *ep.* 105.3, *PL* 54.1000, JW 482; *ep.* 106.5, *PL* 54.1005, 1007, JW 483; *ep.* 110, *PL* 54.1020; *ep.* 114.1, *PL* 54.1029, JW 490; *ep.* 124.1, *PL* 54.1062-63, JW 500.

²³Leo, *ep.* 156.6, *PL* 54.1131, JW 532; *ep.* 139.4, *PL* 54.1107, JW 514; *ep.* 144, *PL* 54.1113, JW 520; *ep.* 145.1, *PL* 54.1114, JW 521.

²⁴Hilary, *ep.* 4.1, in *Epistolae romanorum pontificum genuinae et quae ad eos scriptas sunt a.s. Hilaro usque ad Pelagium II*, vol. I (Braunsberg: E. Peter, 1867; reprinted Hildesheim: G. Olms, 1974), p. 137, JW 552; *ep.* 6.2, Thiel, p. 140, JW 553; *ep.* 8.2, Thiel, p. 143, JW 555; *ep.* 5.1, Thiel, p. 138; *ep.* 10.4, Thiel, p. 150, JW 557; see also H. Burn-Murdoch, *The Development of the Papacy* (London: Faber & Faber, 1954); F. W. Puller, *The Primitive Saints and the See of Rome* (London: Longmans, Green, 1914, 3rd. rev. ed; original, 1893).

²⁵For the Christological issue, see Alois Grillmeier, *Christ in Christian Tradition*, vol. 2, pt. 1 (Atlanta: John Knox Press, 1987); Simplicius, *ep.* 2.2-3, Thiel, pp. 178-79, JW 572, *Collectio Avellana (CA) ep.* 58 (*CSEL* 35); *ep.* 3.4-6, Thiel, pp. 181-82, JW 573, *CA ep.* 56; *ep.* 4.1, Thiel, pp. 183-84, JW 574, *CA ep.* 59; *ep.* 6.2, Thiel, p. 188, JW 576, *CA ep.* 60; *ep.* 5, Thiel, p. 186, JW 575, *CA ep.* 57; *ep.* 6.4, Thiel, pp. 188-89, JW 576, E. Schwartz, *Publizistische Sammlungen zum Acacianischen Schisma*, ABAW 10 (1934) (PS), p. 122; *ep.* 7.5, Thiel, p. 192, JW 577; *ep.* 18.1, Thiel, p. 208, JW 587; *ep.* 20, Thiel, p. 213, JW 589.

[26] Felix, *ep.* 1.3, Thiel, p. 224, JW 591, PS p. 64; *ep.* 1.12, Thiel, pp. 229-30, JW 591; *ep.* 2.1, 3, Thiel, pp. 232-34, JW 592, PS pp. 69-70; *ep.* 3.1, Thiel, p. 239, JW 593; *ep.* 8.4-5, Thiel, pp. 249-50, JW 601.

[27] Felix, *ep.* 17.2, Thiel, pp. 275-76, JW 615, PS p. 79; *ep.* 14.3, Thiel, pp. 267-68, JW 613.

[28] On Gelasius, see Walter Ullmann, *Gelasius I: Das Papsttum an der Wende der Spätantike zum Mittelalter,* Päpste und Papsttum, Bd. 18 (Stuttgart: A. Hiersemann, 1981); S. McGrade, "Two Fifth-Century Concepts of Papal Primacy," *Studies in Medieval and Renaissance History* (Lincoln, Nebraska) 7 (1970), 3-45; J. Taylor, "The Early Papacy at Work: Gelasius I (492-496)," *Journal of Religious History* 8 (1974-75), pp. 317-32.

[29] Gelasius, *ep.* 4.1, Thiel, p. 121, JW 625, *CA ep.* 98 (*CSEL* 35.436-37); *ep.* 30.15, Thiel, p. 447, PS p. 48; *ep.* 18.4, Thiel, p. 384, JW 638; *ep.* 26, Thiel, pp. 392-413, JW 664; *ep.* 3.4, Thiel, p. 314, JW 620, PS p. 50.

[30] Gelasius, *ep.* 3.12, 14, Thiel, pp. 318-19, JW 620, PS pp. 53-55; *ep.* 3.15, Thiel, p. 320, JW 620, PS p. 55; *ep.* 1.1, Thiel, p. 288, JW 611, PS p. 33; *ep.* 26.5, Thiel, pp. 399-400, JW 664; *ep.* 1.9, Thiel, pp. 291-92, JW 611, PS p. 35; *ep.* 1.26, Thiel, p. 302, JW 611, PS p. 42; *ep.* 12.9, Thiel, pp. 356-57, JW 632, PS p. 23.

[31] Gelasius, *ep.* 10.5-6, Thiel, pp. 343-44, JW 622, PS p. 17; *ep.* 10.9, Thiel, p. 347, JW 622, PS pp. 18-19; *ep.* 26.5, Thiel, pp. 399-400, JW 664, *CA ep.* 95, pp. 378-80.

[32] Gelasius, *ep.* 26.5-6, Thiel, pp. 400-01, JW 664, *CA ep.* 95, pp. 380-81; *ep.* 26.10, Thiel, p. 405, JW 664, *CA ep.* 95, p. 387; *ep.* 26.4, 5, 10, Thiel, p. 398, JW 664, *CA ep.* 95, pp. 370-72.

[33] Gelasius, *ep.* 26.16, Thiel, p. 413, JW 664, *CA ep.* 95, p. 398; *ep.* 26.14, Thiel, p. 413, JW 664, *CA ep.* 95, p. 397; *ep.* 27.9-10, Thiel, pp. 431-33, JW 665, PS pp. 29-30; *ep.* 4.2-3, Thiel, pp. 322-23, JW 625, *CA ep.* 98, p. 438; *ep.* 5.2, Thiel, p. 325, JW 626, *CA ep.* 96, p. 400; *ep.* 6.9, Thiel, pp. 333-34, JW 621, *CA ep.* 94, p. 367; *ep.* 8.1, Thiel, p. 338, JW 624, PS p. 57; *ep.* 14.1, 9, Thiel, pp. 362, 367, JW 636.

[34] Gelasius, *ep.* 1.19, Thiel, pp. 297-98, JW 611, PS p. 39; *ep.* 12.3, Thiel, p. 352, JW 632, PS p. 20; *ep.* 18.2, 3, 6, Thiel, pp. 384-85, JW 638, *CA ep.* 101, pp. 465-66, 468; *ep.* 26.3-4, Thiel, pp. 395, 397-98, JW 664, *CA ep.* 95, pp. 372, 375-77; *ep.* 26.1, Thiel, p. 393, JW 664, *CA ep.* 95, pp. 369-70; *tract.* 3.16, Thiel, p. 543, PS p. 95; *tract. de anathema* I, Thiel, pp. 557-58, PS pp. 7-8; *ep.* 3.16, Thiel, pp. 320-21, JW 620, PS p. 55.

[35] Gelasius, *ep.* 7.2, Thiel, p. 335, JW 623, *CA* 79 p. 220; *ep.* 26.9, Thiel, p. 405, JW 664, *CA* 95 pp. 49-52; *ep.* 1.33, 41, Thiel, pp. 305, 310, JW 611, PS pp. 44, 48; *ep.* 1.39, Thiel, p. 310, JW 611, PS p. 47; *ep.* 1.21, Thiel, p. 299, JW 611, PS p. 40; *ep.* 1.27, 34, Thiel, pp. 302, 306, JW 611, PS pp. 42, 44-45; *ep.* 1.42, Thiel, p. 311, JW 611, PS p. 48; *ep.* 3.1, Thiel, pp. 312-13, JW 620, PS p. 49; *ep.* 12.12, Thiel, p. 358, JW 632, PS p. 24; *ep.* 12.5-6, Thiel, p. 353, JW 632, PS p. 21; *ep.* 1.25, Thiel, p. 301, JW 611, PS p. 41.

[36] Gelasius, *ep.* 1.13, Thiel, p. 295, JW 611, PS p. 37; *ep.* 3.15, Thiel, p. 320, JW 620, PS p. 55; *ep.* 12.1, Thiel, p. 350, JW 632, PS p. 19; *ep.* 1.10, Thiel, pp. 292-93, JW 611, PS pp. 35-36.

[37] Gelasius, *ep.* 12.2, Thiel, pp. 350-51, JW 632, PS p. 20; *Liber pontificalis* 52, edited by Louis Duchesne (Paris, 1886).

Chapter VII

[1] On the formula of Hormisdas, see *ep.* 7.9, Thiel pp. 754-55, JW 774, *CA* 89 pp. 338-39 (a letter from Justinian to Pope Agapitus, March 536).

[2] On the reign of Justinian, see A. A. Vasiliev, *Justin the First: An Introduction to the Reign of Justinian the Great* (Cambridge: Harvard University Press, 1950); in general, the works of Procopius of Caesarea in the Loeb Classical Library; on the Three Chapters controversy, E. Amann, "Trois-Chapitres," *Dictionnaire de Théologie Catholique* XV, pt. 2, cc. 1868-1924 (1950); J. Straub, "Die Verurteilung der Drei Kapitel durch Vigilius," *Kleronomia* 2 (1970), 347-75; John of Constantinople to Hormisdas, *ep.* 67.2, Thiel pp. 863-64.

[3] Vigilius, *ep.* 1.7, *PL* 69.19, JW 907; *ep.* 7, *PL* 69.28, JW 913.

[4] Pelagius I, *Pelagii diaconi ecclesiae romanae in defensione trium capitulorum,* ed. Robert Devreesse, Studi e Testi 57 (Vatican City: Biblioteca Vaticana, 1932).

[5] P. M. Gassó and C. M. Batlle, eds., *Pelagii I Papae epistolae quae supersunt* (Montserrat, 1956) (GB); *ep.* 11.10, GB p. 40, JW 938; *ep.* 3.1, GB p. 7, JW 942.

[6] Pelagius, *ep.* 3.4-5, GB pp. 8-9, JW 942; *ep.* 80, GB pp. 196-97, JW 972; *ep.* 38, GB pp. 109-10, JW 971, 997; *ep.* 19.22, 24, GB p. 60, JW 978; *ep.* 11.2, GB p. 36, JW 938; *ep.* 19.1, GB p. 55, JW 978; *ep.* 10, GB pp. 31ff. JW 939; *ep.* 19.17, GB p. 59, JW 978.

[7] Pelagius, *ep.* 24.2-3, GB p. 74, JW 983; *ep.* 24.17, GB p. 77; *ep.* 24.12, GB p. 76; *ep.* 35.13, GB p. 100, JW 994; *ep.* 35.1-2, GB pp. 96-97; *ep.* 35.11, GB p. 99; *ep.* 39, GB pp. 111-12, JW 998; *ep.* 59.2, GB pp. 156-57, JW 1018; *ep.* 59.8-9, GB p. 158.

[8] Pelagius, *ep.* 37, GB pp. 106-8, JW 996, 1007; *ep.* 6.3, GB pp. 18-19, JW 945; *ep.* 8, GB pp. 26-7, JW 948; *ep.* 7.17-18, GB p. 25, JW 946; *ep.* 53, GB pp. 140-42, JW 1012; *ep.* 60.3, GB pp. 160-61, JW 1019; *ep.* 65, GB pp. 171-73, JW 1024; *ep.* 69, GB pp. 178-79, JW 952.

[9] Pelagius, *ep.* 52.5-6, GB p. 136, JW 1011, 1038; *ep.* 52.13ff., GB p. 138, JW 1011, 1038; *ep.* 67, GB p. 175, JW 1026; *ep.* 74, GB p. 188, JW 1032; *ep.* 71, GB p. 182, JW 1029; *ep.* 70, GB pp. 180-81, JW 1028; *ep.* 7.2-3, GB p. 21, JW 946; *ep.* 11.3, 6, GB pp. 36-38, JW 938; *ep.* 10.4, GB p. 33, JW 939; *ep.* 59.6-7, GB pp. 157-58, JW 1018.

[10] Pelagius, *ep.* 19.3, GB p. 56, JW 978; *ep.* 19.17, GB p. 59, JW 978.

[11] Pelagius II, *ep.* 1.5-6, ed. E. Schwartz, *Acta conciliorum oecumenicorum (ACO)* IV.2 p. 105, JW 1054; *ep.* 1.15-16, *ACO* p. 106; *ep.* 1.7-8, *ACO* pp. 105-06; *ep.* 1.13, *ACO* p. 106; *ep.* 2.1-2, *ACO* p. 108, JW 1055; *ep.* 2.20; *ACO* p. 110; *ep.* 2.17-18, *ACO* p. 110; *ep.* 2.9, 13-14, *ACO* pp. 109, 113.

[12] Pelagius II, *ep.* 3.13, *ACO* p. 113, JW 1056; *ep.* 3.38, *ACO* p. 116; *ep.* 3.53, *ACO* p. 118; *ep.* 3.57-59, *ACO* pp. 118-19; *ep.* 3.60-61, *ACO* p. 119.

[13] Pelagius II, *ep.* 3.45, 67ff., *ACO* pp. 117, 120; *ep.* 3.63, *ACO* p. 119; *ep.* 3.84, *ACO* p. 122; *ep.* 3.96, *ACO* pp. 125-26; *ep.* 3.102, 104, *ACO* p. 126; Leo I, *ep.* 119.5, *PL* 54.1045, JW 495; Pelagius II, *ep.* 3.115-19; *ACO* pp. 128-29, JW 1056; *ep.* 3.122, *ACO* p. 129; *ep.* 3.140, 147, *ACO* pp. 130-31.

[14] Gregory I, *ep.* I.16, *CCL* 140.16, JW 1084; *ep.* VIII.4, *CCL* 140A.520-21, JW 1491; *ep.* III.10. *CCL* 140.157-58, JW 1214; *ep.* II.43, *CCL* 140.131-32, JW 1203; *ep.* III.10, *CCL* 140.158, JW 1214; *ep.* IV.3, *CCL* 140.219-220; JW 1274; *ep.* IV.33, *CCL* 140.253, JW 1308; *ep.* XIV.12, *CCL* 140A.1083, JW 1925.

[15] Gregory I, *ep.* II.25, *CCL* 140.111, JW 1181; *ep.* IV.41, *CCL* 140.262, JW 1313;

ep. V.56, *CCL* 140.350-51, JW 1372; *ep.* I.16, *CCL* 140.16, JW 1084; *ep.* IV.14, *CCL* 140.232, JW 1285; *ep.* VI.38, *CCL* 140.412, JW 1418; *ep.* XIII.34, *CCL* 140A.1036, JW 1901; *ep.* IX.187, *CCL* 140A.743, JW 1710; *ep.* II.38, *CCL* 140.123, JW 1198; *ep.* II.43, *CCL* 140.131, JW 1203; *ep.* IX.154, *CCL* 140A.709-10, JW 1679; *ep.* II.43, *CCL* 140.132, JW 1203; *ep.* IX.148, *CCL* 140A.701, JW 1673; *ep.* IX.202, *CCL* 140A.760, JW 1728.

[16]Gregory I, *ep.* IV.2, *CCL* 140.218, JW 1273; *ep.* IV.37, *CCL* 140.257-58, JW 1309; *ep.* IX.148, *CCL* 140A.700-01, JW 1673; *ep.* VI.2, *CCL* 140.370-71, JW 1381.

[17]Columbanus, *Opera,* ed. G. S. M. Walker, Scriptores Latini Hiberniae 2 (Dublin, 1957), *ep.* 5.3, p. 38; *ep.* 5.4-5, p. 40; *ep.* 5.10-11, pp. 46, 48, 50; *ep.* 5.15, pp. 52, 54.

[18]On the credibility problem for the Papacy at this time, see Karl F. Morrison, *Tradition and Authority in the Western Church 300-1140* (Princeton, N.J.: Princeton University Press, 1969), pp. 111-152.

Bibliography

It is curious that, given the presumed Catholic interest in Roman documents, so little has been done in recent times, especially by Roman Catholics, to produce critical texts of the earliest papal letters. Thus most of the time the reader is obliged to return to Jacques Paul Migne's *Patrologia Latina (PL)* for the Latin texts. The man whose critical edition is reprinted in Migne is the eighteenth-century Benedictine monk of St. Germain-des-Prés in Paris, Pierre Coustant (1654-1721), who published his edition of early papal letters in the year of his death. A few recent discoveries or corrections of attributions appear in Adolf Hamman's supplementary volumes to *PL (Patrologiae Latinae Supplementum - PLS)*.

Thus far the current project for publishing new critical editions of patristic texts *Corpus Christianorum series latina (CCL)* has issued only new texts of Leo's sermons (volumes 138 and 138A, edited by A. Chavasse.) There is also a recent edition of the sermons by R. Dolle in *Sources chrétiennes (SC)*, volumes 22, 49, 74, and 200. More recently still, D. Norberg has published a new edition of the letters of Gregory the Great (*CCL* 140, 140A).

A nineteenth-century effort at a critical edition of papal letters after Leo by Andreas Thiel remained unfinished, *Epistolae romanorum pontificum genuinae et quae ad eos scriptae sunt a.s. Hilario usque ad Pelagium II*, volume one. (No others appeared.) (Braunsberg: E. Peter, 1867; repr. Hildesheim: G. Olms, 1974). Critical editions of some letters and of other materials connected with the early ecumenical councils can be found in *Acta conciliorum oecumenicorum (ACO)*, edited by E. Schwartz.

Primary Sources

Damasus (366-384) *PL* 13.347-373; 13.1181-1194 (*ep.* 10); A. Ferrua, *Epigrammata Damasiana* (Verse) (Vatican City, 1942).

Siricius (384-399) *PL* 13.1131-1178; *PLS* 1.567-68.

Anastasius I (399-401) *PL* 20.68-80; *PLS* 1.790-92.

Innocent I (401-417) *PL* 20.463-608; *PLS* 1.793-96; *Ep.* 25, critical edition by Robert Cabié, *La lettre du pape Innocent Ier à Décentius de Gubbio (19 mars 416),* texte critique, traduction et commentaire, *Bibliothèque de la Revue d'histoire ecclésiasti que.* Fs. 58 (Louvain: Presses universitaires, 1973).

[The *Collectio Avellana (CA)* also contains some letters of these popes. A critical edition was published in 1895 by Otto Günther in the Vienna corpus (*CSEL*), vol. 35. *CA* letters 41-44 are Innocent's].

Zosimus (417-18) *PL* 20.642-686; *PLS* 1.796-99; *CA epp.* 45-46, 50.

Boniface I (418-422) *PL* 20.750-784; *PLS* 1.1032-34; *CA epp.* 14-37 concern the dispute over his election.

Celestine (422-432) *PL* 50.417-458; *PLS* 3.18-21; *ACO* I, 1, 7 pp. 125-137, 142-43; I, 2 pp. 5-101.

Sixtus III (432-440) *PL* 50.583-618; *PLS* 3.21-23; *ACO* I, 1, 7 pp. 143-45; I, 2 pp. 107-110.

Leo (440-461) *PL* 54-56 (*epp.* = v. 54); *CA epp.* 51-55; *ACO* II.1-4; *CCL* 138, 138A Sermons (*Tractatus*), ed. A. Chavasse;

selected *epistolae* edited by E. Silva-Tarouca, *Textus et Documenta (Ser. Theol.)* (Rome: Gregorian University, 1932-37).

Hilary (461-468) *PL* 58.11-32; Thiel, pp. 126-174.

Simplicius (468-483) *PL* 58.35-62; Thiel, pp. 175-214; *CA epp.* 56-69.

Felix II (III) (483-492) *PL* 58.893-973; Thiel, pp. 222-227; also, E. Schwartz, ed., *Publizistische Sammlungen zum Acacianischen Schisma* (Transactions of the Bavarian Academy of Sciences, 1934; Heft 10), fourteen letters.

Gelasius (492-496) *PL* 59; *PLS* 3.739-787; Thiel, pp. 285-613; *CA epp.* 79, 81, 94-96, 98, 100-101; Schwartz, *Pub. Samm.* eight letters and two *tractatus.*

Anastasius II (496-498) *PLS* 3.787-797; Thiel, pp. 615-637.

Symmachus (498-514) Thiel, pp. 639-738; *CA ep.* 104.

Hormisdas (514-523) *PL* 63; Thiel, pp. 741-990; *CA epp.* 106, 108, 110, 112, 115-116, 118, 120-124, 126-135, 137, 140, 142, 144-145, 148-158, 168-180, 189, 190, 201-207, 209-211, 219-221, 226-229, 231, 236-240.

John I (523-526) *PL* 59.399-408.

Felix III (IV) *PL* 65.11-16; *ACO* IV, 2 pp. 96-98.

Boniface II (530-532) *PL* 65.31-34.

John II (533-535) *PL* 66.11-26; *CA ep.* 84.

Agapetus I (535-536) *PL* 66.35-80; *CA epp.* 82, 86-88, 91.

Silverius (536-537).

Vigilius (537-555) *PL* 69.15-328; *CA epp.* 83, 92-93; *ACO* I, 3/4 and II, 3, 1/3 concern relevant material from Chalcedon.

Pelagius I (556-561) *PL* 69.393-422; modern editions: *Pelagii I papae epistolae quae supersunt,* ed. Gassó-Batlle (Montserrat, 1956); *Pelagii diaconi "In defensione trium capitulorum",* ed. R. Devreesse (*Studi e Testi,* vol. 57) (Vatican City, 1932).

John III (561-574).

Benedict I (575-579).

Pelagius II (579-590) *PL* 72.703-790; *ACO* IV, 2 (three letters to the bishops of Istria), pp. 105-136.

Gregory I (590-604) *PL* 75-79; *CCL* 140, 140A (*epp.* ed. D. Norberg).

Secondary Sources

Collections of texts relevant to the early history of the Papacy:

C. Mirbt, editor, 6th edition revised by Kurt Aland. *Quellen zur Geschichte des Papsttums und des römischen Katholizismus.* Band 1. Tübingen: J. C. B. Mohr [Paul Siebeck], 1967.

James T. Shotwell and Louise R. Loomis, editors. *The See of Peter.* Records of Civilization, number 7. New York: Columbia University Press, 1927; reprinted: New York: Octagon Books, 1965 (ends with Damasus).

E. Giles. *Documents Illustrating Papal Authority, a.d. 95-454.* London: S.P.C.K., 1952.

H. Burn-Murdoch. *The Development of the Papacy.* London: Faber & Faber, 1954.

General Reference Work:

J. N. D. Kelly. *The Oxford Dictionary of the Popes.* New York: Oxford University Press, 1986.

A. Basic Texts: (see the works referred to above)

Louise Loomis, editor. *The Book of the Popes (Liber Pontificalis) to the Pontificate of Gregory I.* Records of Civilization, number 3. New York: Columbia University Press, 1916; reprinted: New York: Octagon Books, 1965.

R. Davis, editor. *The Book of Pontiffs* (Liverpool: Liverpool University Press, 1989).

B. General Histories:

E. Caspar. *Geschichte des Papsttums.* 2 vols. Tübingen: J. C. B. Mohr (Paul Siebeck), 1930.

A. Franzen & R. Bäumer. *Papstgeschichte.* Freiburg: Herder, 1974.

J. Haller. *Das Papsttum: Idee und Wirklichkeit.* 5 vols. Hamburg: Rowohlt, 1965.

T. Jalland. *The Church and the Papacy.* An historical study. London: S.P.C.K., 1942.

C. Piétri. *Roma Christiana. Recherches sur l'Église de Rome, son organisation, sa politique, son idéologie de Miltiades à Sixte III (311-440).* 2 vols. Paris: de Buccard, 1976.

J. Richards. *The Popes and the Papacy in the Early Middle Ages, 476-752.* London: Rontledge, 1979.

F. Seppelt & G. Schwaiger. *Geschichte der Päpste.* Munich: Kösch, 1964.

E. Weltin. *The Ancient Popes.* Westminster, MD.: Newman Press, 1964.

C. Archeological Questions:

D. O'Connor. *Peter in Rome: the Literary, Liturgical and Archeological Evidence.* New York: Columbia University Press, 1969.

G. Snyder. "Survey and 'New' Thesis on the Bones of Peter." *The Biblical Archeologist* 32, 1 (February 1969), 2-24.

J. E. Walsh. *The Bones of St. Peter.* Garden City, New York: Doubleday & Co., 1982. This is a popularization of debatable conclusions by archeologists; cf. A. G. Martimort, "A propos des reliques de S. Pierre," *Bulletin de littérature ecclésiastique* 87 (1986), pp. 93-112.

D. Saint Peter:

J. Blank. "The Person and Office of Peter in the New Testament." *Concilium* # 83, pp. 42-55.

Raymond Brown, et al., *Peter in the New Testament.* New York: Paulist, 1973.

Oscar Cullmann. *Peter: Disciple, Apostle, Martyr.* Philadelphia: Westminster, 1953.

P. Grelot. "Pierre et Paul, fondateurs de la 'primauté romaine." *Istina* 27 (1982), # 3, pp. 228-268.

O. Karrer. *Peter and the Church: an Examination of Cullmann's Thesis.* New York: Herder & Herder, 1963.

A. LaBonnardière. "Tu es Petrus. La Péricope Matthieu 16.13-23 dans l'oeuvre de St. Augustin." *Irénikon* 34 (1961), pp. 451-499.

E. Lanne. "L'Église de Rome. 'A gloriosissimis duobus apostolis Petro et Paulo Romae fundatae et constitutae ecclesiae' (*Adv. Haer.* III.3.2)." *Irénikon* 49 (1976), pp. 275-322.

Rudolph Pesch. *Simon-Petrus: Geschichte und geschichtliche Bedeutung des ersten Jüngers Jesu Christi.* Päpste und Papsttum 15. Stuttgart: Hiersemann, 1980.

B. Rigaux. "St. Peter in Contemporary Exegesis." *Concilium # 27,* pp. 72-86.

W. Rordorf. "Was heisst: Petrus und Paulus haben die Kirche in Rome 'gegründet'? Zu Irenaeus." *Adv. Haer.* III.1.1; 3, 2.3." *Unterwegs zur Einheit: Festschrift H. Stirnimann,* pp. 609-616. Fribourg: Universitätiverlag, 1980.

T. V. Smith. *Petrine Controversies in Early Christianity: Attitudes toward Peter in Christian Writings of the First Two Centuries.* Wissenschaftliche Untersuchungen zum Neuen Testament. 2. Reihe. Band 15. Tübingen: J. C. B. Mohr [Paul Siebeck], 1985.

R. Staats. "Die martyrologische Begründung des Romprimats bei Ignatius von Antiochien." *Zeitschrift für Theologie und Kirche* 73 (1976), pp. 461-470.

E. General Surveys and Essays:

J. von Allmen, *La Primauté de l'Église de Pierre et de Paul; Remarques d'un Protestant.* Fribourg: Press universitaires, 1977.

P. Batiffol. *Cathedra Petri: Études d'histoire ancienne de l'Église.* Paris: Cerf, 1938 (Collection of earlier essays).

L. Bermejo. "Jurisdictional Primacy by Divine Right: A moot question?" *Bijdragen* 40 (1979), pp. 265-293. (Also: *Toward Christian Reunion* [Anand, India, 1984], pp. 94-133.)

A. Brandenburg & H. J. Urban, eds., *Petrus und Papst.* 2 vols. Münster: Aschendorff, 1977 & 1978.

H. Chadwick. *The Circle and the Ellipse: Rival Concepts of Authority in the Early Church.* Inaugural lecture, Oxford: University Press, 1959.

J. Chapman. *Studies in the Early Papacy.* London, 1928; repr. 1971.

Concilium # 64 (1971, "Papal Ministry in the Church".
    # 108 (1975), "Renouveau ecclésial et service papal à la fin du XXe siècle; (not in the English language edition).

Y. Congar. "Considérations historiques sur la Rupture du 16e siècle dans ses rapports avec la réalisation catholic de l'Unité." *Chrétiens en Dialogue,* pp. 409-435. Paris: Cerf, 1964.

G. Dix. *Jurisdiction in the Early Church, Episcopal and Papal.* London: Faith Press, 1975 (Original, 1938).

P. Empie & A. Murphy, eds., *Papal Primacy and the Universal Church; Teaching Authority and Infallibility in the Church.* Lutherans and Catholics in Dialogue. Vols. 5 & 6. Minneapolis: Augsburg, 1974 & 1980.

C. Ernst. "The Primacy of Peter: Theology and Ideology." *New Blackfriars* 50 (1969), pp. 347-355; 399-404.

U. Gmelin. "Auctoritas, Römisches Princeps und päpstliches Primat," *Geistige Grundlagen römischer Kirchenpolitik.* Stuttgart: Kohlhammer, 1937.

G. Haendler. "Zur Frage nach dem Petrusamt in der alten Kirche." *Studia Theologica* 30 (1976), pp. 89-122.

L. Hertling. *Communio: Church and Papacy in Early Christianity.* Chicago: Loyola University Press, 1972 (Original, 1943).

M. Maccarrone. "Apostolicità, episcopato e primato di Pietro." *Lateranum* 42 (1976).

J. McCue. "The Roman Primacy in the Second Century and the Problem of the Development of Dogma." *Theological Studies* 25 (1964), pp. 161-196.

K. Morrison. *Tradition and Authority in the Western Church, 300-1140.* Princeton University Press, 1969.

G. Schwaiger, ed. *Konzil und Papst: Festschrift H. Tüchle.* Paderborn: F. Schöningh, 1975.

_____. *Päpstlicher Primat und Authorität der allgemeinen Konzilien im Spiegel der Geschichte.* Paderborn: F. Schöningh, 1977.

H. J. Sieben. *Die Konzilsidee der Alten Kirche.* Paderborn: F. Schöningh, 1979.

P. Stockmeier. "Das Petrusamt in der frühen Kirche." *Zum Thema Petrusamt und Papsttum.* Stuttgart: KBW, 1970. See esp. pp. 61-79.

J. M. Tillard. *The Bishop of Rome.* Wilmington: M. Glazier, 1983 (French original, 1982).

C. Vogel. "Communion et Église locale aux premiers siècles. Primatialité et synodalité durant la periode antenicéene." *Année Canonique* 25 (1981), pp. 169-177.

W. de Vries. *Orient et Occident: Les structures ecclésiales vues dans l'histoire des sept premiers conciles oecuméniques.* Paris: Cerf, 1974 (A collection of articles originally published in German from 1967 to 1973).

P. Winter. *St. Peter and the Popes.* Baltimore: Helicon, 1960.

M. Wojtowytsch. *Papsttum und Konzilien von den Anfängen*

bis zu Leo I (440-461). Studien zur Entstehung der überordnung des Papstes über Konzile. Päpste und Papsttum 17. Stuttgart: Hiersemann, 1981, (Critical comment by S. O. Horn in *Annuarium Historiae Conciliorum* 1985).

F. Studies Concerning Particular Individuals, Areas, or Texts:

Mélanges Lambert Beauduin: l'Église et les Églises: 1054-1954. Chevetogne (in vol. 1).

  G. Bardy, "Alexandrie, Antioche, Constantinople (325-451)," pp. 183-207.

  H. Marot. "Les conciles romains des 4e et 5e siècles et le developpement de la Primauté," pp. 209-240.

  C. Moeller. "Reflexions sur les schismes à l'époque des premiers conciles," pp. 241-260.

  D. Amand de Mendieta. "Damase, Athanase, Pierre, Mélèce et Basile," pp. 261-277.

A. Benoit. "St. Irénée et l'Unité de l'Église." *Oecumenica* 2 (1967), pp. 11-20.

H. C. Brennecke. "Rom und der dritte Kanon von Serdika (342)*." *Zeitschrift der Savigny-Stiftung für Rechtsgeschichte (Kan. Abt.)* 69 (1983), pp. 15-45.

N. Brox. "The Conflict between Anicetus and Polycarp." *Concilium* # 71, pp. 37-45.

_____. "Probleme einer Frühdatierung des römischen Primats." Kairos 18 (1976), pp. 81-99.

_____. "Rom und 'jede Kirche' im 2. Jahrhundert." *Annuarium Historiae Conciliorum* 7 (1975), pp. 42-78.

_____. "Tendenzen und Parteilichkeiten im Osterfeststreit des 2. Jahrhunderts." *Zeitschrift für Kirchengeschichte* 83 (1972), pp. 291-324.

P. Conte. *Chiesa e Primato nelle Lettere dei Papi del Secolo VII.* Milan: Vita e Pensievo, 1971.

A. Davids. "One or None: Cyprian on the Church and Tradition." *Concilium* # 71, pp. 46-52.

Robert Eno. "Doctrinal Authority in St. Augustine." *Augustinian Studies* 12 (1981), pp. 133-172.

—————. "Doctrinal Authority in the African Ecclesiology of the Sixth Century: Ferrandus and Facundus." *Revue des Études Augustiniennes* 22 (1976), pp. 95-113.

—————. "*Ecclesia Docens:* Doctrinal Authority in Tertullian and Vincent." *The Thomist* 40 (1976), pp. 96-115.

—————. "Origen and the Church of Rome." *American Ecclesiastical Review* 167 (1973), pp. 41-50.

—————. "Pope and Council: the Patristic Origins." *Science et Esprit* 28 (1976), pp. 183-211.

—————. "Some Elements in the Pre-History of Papal Infallibility." *Teaching Authority and Infallibility in the Church.* Lutherans and Catholics in Dialogue, vol. 6 (1980), pp. 238-258; 344-351. (Minneapolis: Aubsburg, 1980).

—————. "The Work of Optatus as a Turning-Point in the African Ecclesiology." *The Thomist* 37 (1973), pp. 668-685.

W. H. C. Frend. "Eastern Attitudes to Rome during the Acacian Schism." *The Orthodox Churches and the West,* pp. 69-82. Studies in Church History 13. Oxford: Blackwell, 1976.

S. O. Horn. *Petrou Kathedra: Der Bischof von Rom und die Synoden von Ephesus und Chalcedon.* Paderborn: Bonifatius Verlag, 1982.

T. Jalland. *The Life and Times of St. Leo the Great.* London: S.P.C.K. 1941.

P. Joannou. *Die Ostkirche und die Cathedra Petri im 4. Jahrhundert.* Päpste und Papsttum 3. Stuttgart: Hiersemann, 1972. (See also the critical remarks of W.

de Vries in *Orientalia Christiana Periodica* [Rome] 40 [1974], pp. 114-144.)

J. F. Kelly. "The Irish Monks and the See of Peter." *Monastic Studies* 14 (1983), pp. 207-24.

B. Kriegbaum. "Afrikanische Autonomie und römischer Primat. Kanon 8 der römischen Synode von 386 und seine Geltung in Afrika." *Festschrift Fr. Kempf,* pp. 11-21. (Sigmaringen: Thorbecke, 1983).

P. Lampe. *Die stadtrömischen Christen in der ersten beiden Jahrhunderten: Untersuchungen zur Sozialgeschichte.* Wissenschaftliche Untersuchungen zum Neuen Testament. 2. Reihe. Band 18. Tübingen: J. C. B. Mohr [Paul Siebeck], 1987.

G. Langgärtner. *Die Gallienpolitik der Päpste.* Theophaneia, Band 16. Bonn: Peter Hanstein, 1964.

G. LaPiana. "The Roman Church at the End of the Second Century." *Harvard Theological Review* 18 (1925), pp. 201-277.

P. L'Huillier. "Ecclesiology in the Canons of the First Nicene Council." *St. Vladimir's Seminary Theological Quarterly* 27 (1983), pp. 119-131.

S. McGrade. "Two Fifth-century Conceptions of Papal Primacy." *Studies in Medieval and Renaissance History* (Lincoln, Nebraska) 7 (1970), pp. 3-45.

P. McShane. *La Romanitas et le Pape Léon le Grand.* Montréal: Bellarmin, 1979.

L. Magi. *La Sede Romana nella corrispondenza degli imperatori e patriarchi bizantini (6-7 sec.).* Louvain: Publications universitaires, 1972.

W. Marschall. *Karthago und Rom: Die Stellung der nordafrikanischen Kirche zum apostolischen Stuhl in Rom.* Päpste und Papsttum 1. Stuttgart: Hiersemann, 1971.

J. Meyendorff, *et al. The Primacy of Peter in the Orthodox*

Church. London: Faith Press, 1963.

V. Monachino. "Communio e Primato nella Controversia Ariana." *Archivum Historiae Pontificiae* 7 (1969), pp. 43-78.

─────── . "Il Primato nella Controversia Ariana." *Miscellanea Historiae Pontificiae* 21 (1959), pp. 17-89.

─────── . "Il Primato nella Scisma Donatista." *Archivum Historiae Pontificiae* 2 (1964), pp. 7-44.

C. Munier. "La Tradition littéraire des Dossiers Africains." *Revue de Droit Canonique* 29 (1979), pp. 41-52.

P. O'Connell. *The Ecclesiology of St. Nicephorus I (758-828): Pentarchy and Primacy.* Orientalia Christiana Analecta 194. Rome: Oriental Institute, 1972.

I. Ortiz de Urbina. "Patres Graeci de Sede Romana." *Orientalia Christiana Periodica* 29 (1963), pp. 25-51.

H. J. Sieben. *"Sanctissimi Petri apostoli memoriam honoremus.* Die Sardicensischen Appellationskanones im Wandel der Geschichte." *Theologie und Philosophie* 58 (1983), pp. 501-534.

V. Twomey. *Apostolikos Thronos: The Primacy of Rome as reflected in the Church History of Eusebius and the historico-apologetic writings of St. Athanasius the Great.* Münsterische Beiträge zur Theologie, Band 49. Münster: Aschendorff, 1982.

W. Ullmann. *Gelasius I. (492-496): Das Papsttum an der Wende der Spätanike zum Mittelalter.* Päpste und Papsttum 18. Stuttgart: Hiersemann, 1981.

─────── . "Leo I and the Theme of Papal Primacy." *Journal of Theological Studies,* n.s. 11 (1960), pp. 25-51.

O. Wermelinger. *Rome und Pelagius.* Päpste und Papsttum 7. Stuttgart: Hiersemann, 1975.

P. Zmire. "Recherches sur la Collégialté épiscopale dans l'Église d'Afrique." *Recherches Augustiniennes* 7 (1971), pp. 1-72.

G. Related Areas, especially Ecclesiology:

Y. Congar & B. Dupoy, eds. *L'Épiscopat et l'Église universelle.* Paris: Cerf, 1962. Especially:

> H. Marot, "Unité de l'Église et Diversité géographique aux premiers siècles," pp. 565-590;
> C. Vogel, "Unité de l'Église et Pluralité des formes historiques d'organisation ecclésiastiques du IIIe au Ve siècle," pp. 591-636.

Y. Congar. "St. Paul et l'Autorité de l'Église romaine d'apres la Tradition." *Studiorum Paulinorum Congressus Internationalis Catholicus,* vol. I, pp. 491-516. Rome: Biblical Institute, 1963.

_____. "The Historical Development of Authority in the Church." *Problems of Authority,* ed. J. Todd. Baltimore: Helicon, 1962.

_____. *Diversity and Ecclesial Communion* (Mystic, CT.: Twenty-third Publications, 1985).

_____. "Ecclesiological Awareness in the East and in the West from the Sixth to the Eleventh Century." *The Unity of the Churches of God,* ed. P. Sherwood, pp. 127-184. Baltimore: Helicon, 1962.

_____. *L'Église de St. Augustin à l'époque moderne.* Paris: Cerf, 1970.

_____. *L'Ecclésiologie du Haut Moyen Age.* Paris: Cerf, 1968. F. Dvornik. *Byzantium and the Roman Primacy.* New York: Fordham University Press, 1966.

_____. *The Idea of Apostolicity in Byzantium and the Legend of the Apostle Andrew.* Washington: Dumbarton Oaks, 1958.

S. Greenslade. *Schism in the Early Church.* 2nd. ed. London: SCM Press, 1964.

G. Hudon. "L'Église dans la Pensée de Saint Léon." *Église et Théologie* 14 (1983), pp. 305-336.

H. Küng. *The Church,* esp. pp. 444-480. New York: Sheed & Ward, 1968.

J. Lécuyer. *Études sur la Collégialité épiscopale.* Le Puy: X. Moppus, 1964.

H. Marot. "La Collégialité et le Vocabulaire épiscopal du Ve au VIIe siècle." *La Collégialité épiscopale,* pp. 59-98. Paris: Cerf, 1965.

————. "The Primacy and the Decentralization of the Early Church." *Concilium* # 61, pp. 9-16.

G. Roethe. "Zur Geschichte der römischen Synoden im 3. und 4. Jahrhunderte." *Geistige Grundlagen der römischen Kirchenpolitik.* Stuttgart: Kohlhammer, 1937.

An Annual bibliography on the papacy appears in the *Archivum Historiae Pontificiae* (Rome).

Subject Index

Modern Authors and Popes

Subject Index

Ancient Names